Life Begins
Kids Leave Home
And The Dog Dies

BARB TAUB

LIFE BEGINS WHEN THE KIDS LEAVE HOME AND THE DOG DIES
Copyright © 2018 Barb Taub

ISBN: 9781976934124

Dedication

To all those who shared their wisdom with me: if I'd listened, what would I have to write about?

A priest, a minister and a rabbi were talking about when life begins. The priest said: "Life begins at conception." The minister said: "Life begins when the fetus is viable." The rabbi said: "Life begins when the kids leave home and the dog dies."

While this joke has innumerable versions, this is the one Great-Uncle Herbie told when we got married. He and Great-Aunt Fanny also told us not to eat in restaurants with plants (they're put there to hide something), not to give each other presents with handles, and especially not to not let our kids outnumber us.

This book documents results of breaking every one of Great-Uncle Herbie's life rules. I like to think he would have approved.

❖ ❖ ❖

Because It Really Is All About Me

[NOTE from Barb: Lots of books have the author's biography in there somewhere. This is my book, so I'm putting my bio right at the beginning. Because I can.]

Once Upon a Time

Chapter 1

A girl met her prince. He was tall, dark, and handsome. (Actually, he was a Republican. But he was definitely tall.) They fell in love, and got married.*

Chapter 2.

He brought her to his castle and they lived happily ever after.**

THE END**

Luckily, thirty-five+ years of life happened between Chapters 1 and 2, or I'd have nothing to write about. They included:

MONTHS	SPENT:
36	Pregnant
96	Changing diapers
192	Getting offspring into or out of carseats
180	Driving to Sunday School
48 bazillion	Driving practice with teenage drivers. (Note: this item is multiplied by Parental-Terror units, which include the number of times your life flashes before your eyes…)
134 down, 10 to go	College tuition

360	Thinking up something to have for dinner
0	Playing with my grandchildren (but I'm not bitter. Much…)

** *In the romance-writing biz, we aim for the HEA (Happily-Ever-After), or—if we're milking it for series potential—at least a HFN (Happily-for-Now. No, it doesn't mean Hell-eFfing-No…).*

I was thinking about the HFN when I went to a friend's birthday lunch. She's 93, so I asked her to tell me about her favorite birthday ever. "Considering the alternative," she told me, "Every birthday I make it to is the best one ever." So of course, I asked for her secret to a long Happy Ever After. She answered right away. "Have a lot of friends who remember you even when you can't remember their names." A few minutes later she added, "Don't say no to sweets." And finally, "Don't look back."

*** UPDATES: So actually my Chapter 2 was just a HFN, and we're well into Chapter 3:

- We've downsized from the castle in England, to the Hobbit House in Scotland, to a very needy Victorian on an island off the coast of Scotland. Hint: *What do Scots wear under their kilts?* I now know!

- The College Tuition entry can now move to 144 down, 0 to go.

And the best update of Chapter 3? I can change that last line of the chart to read:

YEARS: 2   *SPENT*: Playing with my grandchild

Grandparenting rocks. Turns out that Chapter 3 is the real HEA!

❖ ❖ ❖

CONTENTS

Table of Contents

Acknowledgments

This is the part where I thank my family, pets, friends, and total strangers for just being so hilarious I couldn't help writing about you. And, while I'm eternally grateful to each of you—you know who you are!—there is another group who are far more responsible for this book. My readers. You are the generous, funny, responsive, humorous souls who've read, laughed, commented, occasionally snorted coffee over your monitor, and then read more. I wish I could give each of you a hug, but...well, there are laws about that sort of thing. So instead, here is your book. I hope you like it.

PART 1: KIDS

♦♦♦

Chapter 1: Serial Kid-Producer Reveals Top 10 Reasons Not To Have Kids

There are actually LOTS of reasons not to have kids. As a serial kid-producer, I offer a curated list:

10. Vermin = Pet: For me the word "rodent" evokes two images.

#1. Life-enhancing scientific research seeking the cure for cancer and the perfect makeup foundation base.

#2. Plague-spreading vermin.

(Or three images if you don't include presidential candidates in #2 above.)

But your children will love all rodents, from Anatole "The bravest mouse in France" to Mickey "The richest mouse in pants". When we lived in Virginia, some local field mice decided to go on the Taub rodent-welfare system. So I bought some standard mousetraps and baited them with cheese and peanutbutter. Then I threw them away.

> [*NOTE: Anyone who actually uses this type of trap to catch Cinderella's tiny helpers is welcome to explain to children that it works by breaking Feivel, Miss Bianca, Bernard, and even Mighty Mouse's little backs. While you're at it, you can tell them who is going to take care of all of Hunca Munca's baby mousies now.*]

I'll bet the people who invented the better mousetrap weren't looking for the world to beat a path to their door. (The World leaves such a mess on the front walkway…) They just wanted to look their kids in the eye again. That's how we felt when we bought the Have-A-Heart mousetraps. The way these work is every night for weeks you load up the ends of the traps with a three-course gourmet rodent feast—peanutbutter, cheese, and chocolate chips. Each night, the delighted rodents rush into the traps, eat everything, burp at the cat, and leave. Finally they get so obese they trip the little trap-door. Then your husband and kids take a long walk into the fields behind your house. They open the trap and coo over the mouse when he waddles out.

The humanely-trapped mouse tells all his little mousie buddies about this great house where they feed you every night and then take you for a lovely ride. The rodent and his pals probably make it back to your house before your husband and kids.

9. Credibility Gap: Your children won't believe you when you tell them:

- The world is round.
- Vegetables are good.
- Nice children share instead of fighting to determine who gets the toy. (Or the TV remote. Or to be on top. Or Afghanistan.)
- You need to learn long division even if you're going to be a professional athlete or movie star. (BTW: your children probably also won't believe there's such a thing as calculus in the real world. I think they're right on that one.)
- This hurts me more than it hurts you.
- Your cat/ dog/ rodent/ goldfish is going away to live on a farm.

This inability to accept adult realities goes a long way toward explaining such phenomena as Cubs fans, 'lite' cheesecake, and Republican presidential candidates.

My own credibility wasn't helped by my disposal of my children's beloved playroom couch. When the legs of The World's Ugliest Sofa** collapsed, my first reaction was there is a God and prayer works.

> **[I realize some readers may dispute the sofa's right to that title. But consider: does your ugly sofa weigh more than a pair of sumo wrestlers? Does it sport 12-inch high depictions of the Spirit of '76 in bloody colored detail? Or make regular appearances in your worst nightmares? I rest my case.]*

I told the kids we were giving their sofa to a poor family who couldn't afford to buy an ugly sofa of their own. Unfortunately, Goodwill refused to accept the sofa out of humanitarian concern for its clientele. The kids arrived outside just in time to see their beloved sofa loaded onto a disposal truck and *run through its shredder*.

I realized just how low my credibility had dipped when I was reminiscing recently about going to a huge amount of trouble to find a new home for the cat when my son turned out to be allergic to her. The people who adopted her actually *did* live on a farm, and they said there were plenty of mice for her to chase in their barn. Really. But in the twenty years since we told our children we were sending the cat to live on a mouse farm, not one of my children has ever wavered in their absolute certainty that the mouse farm was located in the same place that the sofa ended up.

8. National holidays: Before kids, you celebrate New Years at midnight. You still do after kids, but you just use a midnight that's already happened. Living in the Midwest, we started with New York. By Child#2, we were using England. By Child#4, Australia was looking good.

7. Sleep: My own children elevated parental sleep deprivation to an Olympic event. On any given night, I could be awakened at 0-dark:30 by a small person climbing into my bed, putting little arms around my neck, and confiding, "I hafta throw up." I think the kids had time-trials to see how fast parents could be roused from a dead stupor.

6. Money: Money is even harder to get than sleep. Face it, eventually you will get some sleep, usually during a nonessential activity like driving to work. But a fundamental rule of child-rearing is that you will never again have any money. You may think you can manage to pay for orthodontia, shoes your child outgrows on the way home from the shoe store, and pediatric antibiotics that cost more per ounce than your engagement ring. All you have to do is give up luxuries like eating *every* night and concentrate on essentials like babysitters. To you I say–college. CNBC projects the cost for your newborn to attend a private university in 18 years will be $130,428. Per *year*.

5. Sex: Contrary to popular opinion, people who commit parenthood still have sex. They just have to do it really quietly. And really really quickly.

4. Illness: Your children will think prescription Pink Stuff is one of the basic food groups. You will think it might be cheaper to install your child in one of those germ-barrier bubbles. Pharmaceutical executives vacationing in the South of France will think it's great that you're sending *their* children to Ivy League colleges.

3. Travel: Think of every wonderful trip you've ever wanted to take. Fabulous food? Exotic beaches? Exciting slopes? Forget it. Your kids will only be interested in one trip. If you're not taking them to the Mouse, it will be a lot easier to pitch a tent in your back yard and drive to Chez Macs three times a day. (The bad news is that there is absolutely. No. Escape. If you have children, you WILL do the Mouse. I'm so sorry.)

2. More kids: Your first child is your gateway drug. You may think you can stop any time, but all of a sudden you're talking about how it's not 'fair' for your baby to grow up as an only child. If you weren't suffering from sleep-deprivation delusions, you would realize that every child firmly believes the universe can only have one center, and she already occupies that position.

1. Top Reason Not to Have Kids? Self esteem: If any self esteem managed to survive labor and delivery (where every medical person and possibly a few passersby had a hand–usually literally–in getting you to push a watermelon out an opening the size of a plum), you can kiss it goodbye by the time your first child becomes verbal. Not realizing that the chief purpose of encouraging baby talk is to keep the child unintelligible for as long as possible, we were careful to teach clear enunciation and precise terminology, allowing our children to deliver publicly humiliating statements at will.

For example, I pinched my two-year-old's neck in the top of her coat zipper once. Toward the end of church services the next day, I tried to take advantage of a lull to put her coat on her. "Mommy," she shrieked amid the hushed pews, "Don't hurt me again!" We had to look for a new congregation.

Another time we had stopped for some toddler haute cuisine at Chez Big Mac when my other daughter inquired in ringing tones, "Mommy, why is that person so ugly?"

"That's not a nice thing to say," I hissed back in my best parental fury whisper.

"But, Mommy..."

"No."

"But, Mommy, I was only..."

"NO!"

"But, Mommy!" She was sobbing now. "I wasn't going to ask again why that person is SO UGLY."

"OK, what?" I relented.

"Mommy, WHY IS THAT UGLY PERSON SO FAT?"

Then there was the time the two-year-old asked me where her tail was. I explained that children don't have tails.

"Michael does," she stated and pointed.

I immediately explained about male and female plumbing differences. She was fascinated, and the next several days were spent speculating–loudly–on who had what where. This interesting period culminated in a visit to a crowded local restaurant where she was inspired to stand up on her chair and announce–at full volume to a spellbound roomful of diners–what MY daddy has and what MY mommy has. This time, we moved to another town.

When people ask me why, despite the above list, we produced kids-x-four, I usually tell them we were doing our part to improve the gene pool. But the truth is a bit different. Like someone who suddenly realizes they can breathe underwater, I figured out that I could actually live without sleep, money, or a clean house for the next couple of decades. And that it's all worth it to watch as the four most amazing people ever born grow up.

Even if they do think I killed their cat.

◆ ◆ ◆

Chapter 2: Okay, Kids: That's $2,025,304 You Owe Me. I'll Take A Check. Or Maybe A Grandchild…

When I told my sister we were completely remodeling our bathroom, she asked me if we were rich. I told her two things.

<u>Thing One</u>: Rich people rarely have this as their "before" picture.

Do NOT make me tell you about the bucket. Let's just pretend it's a decorative accent in our early-armageddon theme…

Thing Two: We committed parenthood. Four times, actually. According to the U.S. Department of Agriculture's 2013 report, the cost of raising a child is $506,326 per kid. That comes to $2,025,304. Before taxes.

And we're not alone. According to informed sociological sources such as the supermarket publication containing the interesting information that Elvis had returned in a UFO to sire a British royal heir, the cost of baby production and maintenance has raised biological clock-ticking angst to alarming heights.

I've given this situation a lot of thought, and for humanitarian reasons and the vast sums of money my other writing is NOT generating, I've decided to provide you with the benefit of my own child-rearing expertise and expenses. After all, I've got four children and none of us has yet been convicted of a major felony. (Although it was touch and go while my son was in preschool…)

If you don't count worrying about your child eating one of those little button batteries and needing a rush batteryectomy before stomach acid meets battery acid, the only two things new parents have to worry about are money and sleep. At the birth of your child, you can kiss both goodbye.

For parents, of course, money is even harder to get than sleep. Face it, eventually you will get some sleep, usually during a nonessential activity like driving to work. But a fundamental rule of childrearing is that you will never again have any money. The following alarming statistics drawn randomly from just the first five years will give you an idea of how the rule works:

- You'll spend $1,250 on about 7,280 disposable diapers. This is enough to fill City Hall with the soiled ones. (Which, if the wind doesn't shift, is actually not a bad idea when you think about it…)

- Because of a little-understood phenomenon we experts call the BabyGap effect, you cannot buy enough clothes for your child. For example: you go to the mall one morning and buy this winter's toddler wardrobe. You then stop at Chez Big Mac, where the child who has not eaten since July 4th consumes three entire Kids Meals (holding out her tongue for you to remove stray pickles and onions of course) and knocks back a quart of ketchup. You arrive home to find your child has grown two sizes too large for the morning's purchases, none of which can be returned because she stored the de-tongued pickles and onions from McLunch in the shopping bags.)

- You'll spend $912.50 for the 1,823 quarts of milk your child will pour directly onto the floor and another $9,100 on food which your child will refuse to eat because it is a) green or b) not green.

- You'll spend $1,350 on graham crackers, none of which your child will actually consume. Mixed with baby saliva, they will form a layer on the seat of your car which is impervious to any known human tool. NASA is experimenting with using family car backseats as future heat shields on upcoming space missions.

- Your child will flush the toilet 10,950 times, using 131,412 gallons of water. You may argue that you get a break from flushing for the first two years. This is entirely offset, however, by that stage where the spirit of scientific adventure will move your toddler to unroll about five pounds of toilet paper into the basin and then flush. Repeatedly. Besides destroying every bit of plumbing in your house, this generally tends to neutralize the survival benefits of being extremely cute, frequently all that stands between a two-year-old and justifiable homicide.

- You'll buy 173 pairs of shoes, not one of which will actually fit. This is because brilliant shoe scientists at the Foreign Shoe Institute have developed material which actually shrinks new shoes 2 1/2 sizes when warmed to toddler body temperature as your child wears them out of the store. At a cost per linear inch, these children's shoes rank right up there with the rarer gems and the Pentagon's newest bomber program.

- Your child will have 127 ear infections which will cost $9,178 in doctor office visits because they will only develop symptoms during the holiday and weekend rate hours, or on national holidays. This is nothing compared to the gallons of prescription antibiotic which will cost about as much as mounting your own space program.

You parents may think that despite all this, you can get by if you make a few sacrifices. You can give up such luxuries as eating *every* night and concentrate on bare essentials like baby sitters. To you I say one word. College.

There is an adage that a year of college costs about as much as a new Ford. Well, there is a much bigger selection of Fords today than when old Henry F. said people could have any color they wanted as long as it was black. And there is an equally wide spectrum in college tuitions. Whether you want to send your offspring to Harvard (fully tricked-out Ford Expedition EL Platinum) or to the University of Illinois (Ford Fiesta, stripped), saving for the sheepskin is a frightening thought.

I checked with my own alma mater, the University of Chicago. The nice lady in Undergrad Admissions offered information, sympathy, and advice. She said we could project a six-percent yearly increase in college costs from the $19,275 cost the year we started our baby production run. Thus a newborn's diploma in the class of 2011 would run a mere $240,617.15. **[note from Barb: scary accurate prediction]** With four children to send, our bill would come to

9

$962,468.60 or about two-thirds of our annual income until 2217 if we start saving immediately and stop buying pediatric antibiotics.

Although invoicing my kids gave me something to occupy my mind during the midnight shifts of child maintenance, I sometimes think I should have taken the Fords…

But back to my sister's question about whether we're rich. *[See how I wrapped us back around to the beginning of this piece? This is called closure, which I can do because I'm a professional writer. Do not try this at home, boys and girls.]*

"Hell, yeah!" I told my sister. "All four of my children are off the payroll, and nobody wakes me up at night to tell me they have to throw up. You bet I'm rich!"

❖ ❖ ❖

Chapter 3: Parenting: This Is Nothing We Ever Trained For

My mother's hair is getting pretty grey. As she has 10 children, I can't figure out why it has taken her this long. I myself can identify the source of each of my well-deserved and rapidly multiplying silver threads. Take the events of a typical morning like November 7th:

2:37a.m:–The 3-year-old wakes up ready to party. After some discussion, he decides it would be easier to keep our attention if he joins us in our bed.

6:00a.m:–I wake up the 7-year-old who has an early school bus to catch and am joined in the kitchen by the 5-year-old who doesn't have to be up for another hour and a half. She demands waffles. I tell her we don't have any waffles. She sadly informs a bowl of oatmeal that a loving parent would stock better cereal, like those chocolate-chip mini-donuts that glow in the dark.

6:10 am (and 6:15, 6:22 and 6:25a.m.):–Even sending in the shock troops (3-year-old and puppy) fails to blast the 7-year-old out of bed. I carry her into the kitchen, tape open her eyelids, and put her on a chair in front of some oatmeal. No, we don't have any waffles. Eat it.

6:27a.m.–She completes her minute study of the congealing properties of the untouched bowl of oatmeal and retires to the bathroom.

6:51a.m.–I brush her hair and make the lunch we both know she won't eat because I keep putting wholesome things in there in case of a spot-check by the Motherhood Wholesomeness Patrol disguised as lunchroom monitors. (What? Didn't you know the MWP reports back to the Teachers' Lounge things like,

"Barb's kid got some good wholesome stuff to throw into the garbage while little Joey Smith was forced to eat every crumb of his six Chocolate Whammy Wallbangers"?)

7:05a.m.–She can't find her backpack and her shoes. I find them and zip her into her coat despite her protests that nobody in the second grade zips their coat, and I complete her humiliation by forcing her to wear her hat. She goes out the door, unzips the coat, loses the hat, and somehow catches the bus.

8:20a.m.–I drive the 5-year-old to the special kindergarten we are sending her to so she can learn brain surgery in two different languages. (Three, if you count pig-latin.)

10:20a.m.–I call my husband and remind him that we're due at the kindergarten music recital at eleven and I'll pick him up on my way if he's waiting outside because I can't stand to be late. I'm late, and don't have time to stop for gas in my ancient station wagon which gets almost 2 ½ miles to the gallon.

11:00a.m.–Three and a half of the cutest minutes you've ever seen. Their cover of *"Chicken Lips and Lizard Hips"* will definitely be Grammy material, and probably go viral once the video comes out.

11:06a.m.–We get one block from the school and run out of gas. My husband sprints the five blocks to his van and comes back for the 3-year-old, the dog, and me. We drop him off and go to the gas station, where I leave every cent I have in ransom for their ancient gas can. I go back to my illegally abandoned car and attempt to put the gas into it. At this point, I discover that the gas can's nozzle is merely a decorative accent, not attached to the actual can at any point. Necessity being the mother of stupidity, I fasten the nozzle on with strapping tape.

Did you know that strapping tape dissolves in gasoline? I now know that too. By accident, a small amount of gas actually goes into the tank. Smelling exotically of the remaining 1 ½ gallons of eau-de-petrol which I'm now wearing, we head back to return the gas can. While I'm arguing with the attendant about the nozzle-less condition of the gas can, I notice him staring, slack-jawed, over my shoulder. I look behind me and see that the van is gone.

Those of you who aren't shocked to hear this know, of course, that I left the 3-year-old in the car. Testosterone poisoning has taken over, forcing him to escape from the car seat (which takes a college graduate several minutes to unfasten), release the emergency brake, and back the van out across four lanes of traffic, where it sits, broadside.

Both the 3-year-old and the dog are inside, totally fascinated.

"Grace-under-pressure" being my motto, I gracefully drop the gas can and race into traffic, screaming, "*OH. MY. GOOOOOOOODDDD!*" at the top of my lungs. Enchanted with this performance, the attendant returns all my money, obviously realizing that I will need it during the years of intensive psychiatric treatment ahead.

◆ ◆ ◆

Chapter 4: Olympic Gold[En] Moms & Memories

I brought the TV down from the attic and enshrined it in the playroom so my family could cheer our hometown hero, Bonnie Blair, to her latest two Olympic gold medals.

"Mama," my kids wanted to know. "Did you ever win any gold medals?"

I had to tell them the truth. There are three reasons I never won any gold medals:

1. No force on earth or the Marvel universe could make me appear in public wearing skintight spandex.

2. The Hub gets cranky when I try to smuggle the cat into bed, so I'm pretty sure he wouldn't be down with sleeping with my luge sled.

3. Although I have been training night and day for more than ten years, motherhood is not yet an Olympic event.

At least my mother's generation had the *Queen for a Day* show, in which contestants vied to be the most pathetic.

Contestant: "Well, my husband broke both arms and had his legs amputated and just hasn't been the same since the shock therapy and my child needs an operation to fix her eyes so she can compete for Mini-Miss America and the dog has cancer of the tail and I lost my night job at the sweatshop when I got TB so the bank repossessed the house and now we're all living in a cardboard box under the freeway overpass. But I always try to look on the bright side of life."

If the Audience Applause Meter rated her the most pitiful, she won a dryer.

All my generation has is the Pillsbury Bake-Off, and half the time that's won by some man who probably doesn't know the first thing about stretch marks. Or dryers.

But if the Olympic Committee is looking for some events to round out the schedule for the next games, I'd like to suggest they let mothers compete. And it could bring in more sponsors too. Just imagine, The Official Disposable Diaper of Team USA...

For moms who want to get a head start, I have a few tips:

Tip #1. Equipment: Many trainees overestimate the amount of equipment they'll need to stay competitive. Before you purchase any piece of training equipment, I recommend the PFT (The Pioneer Foremothers Test). It's actually quite simple: "Would our pioneer foremothers have needed this?" For example, in our house in the last few weeks we have broken and not yet replaced the following items which did NOT pass the PFT—

- *Hair-dryer*. Our pioneer foremothers did not use hair dryers. In winter they had a choice of frozen braids or not washing their hair until the spring thaws. The latter helped keep away the bears, and (if it was a particularly long winter) the pioneer forefathers.

- *Car battery*. Do think the hardy pioneer foremother was stopped by a dead battery? She would just grab her bonnet, her shawl, and her pioneer forehusband's car.

- *Dishwasher*. Our pioneer foremothers didn't need dishwashers. That's what they had pioneer forechildren for.

- *Oven*. Since pioneer foremothers here on the prairie fueled their ovens with buffalo chips—yes, those are *exactly* what you're picturing—the pioneer forefamily was delighted when the oven broke and they could send out for pizza. Often, while our pioneer foremothers were out in the fields plowing and/or giving birth, the rest of the pioneer forefamily— desperate for food that didn't smell like the wrong end of a buffalo— would sneak in and break the oven themselves.

- *Toilet*. She would just dig a new pioneer forehole.

As I see it, the only essential pieces of training equipment for Olympic Mothering (assuming that the valium wouldn't pass the drug screening) are a coffee pot, a covered wagon/minivan, and a dependable pizza takeout. For those without a buffalo, I also recommend a microwave.

Tip #2. Training: As any athlete will tell you, the most important element here is your state of mind. For the competing mother, this means GUILT. My friend Susan claims that being the cultural heiress to 3000+ years of Jewish mothers gives her an insurmountable guilt lead. But I think there is still room for the talented amateur who is willing to nurture her neuroses about jobs, pottying, and teen-age sex.

Tip #3. Team Uniforms: How about loose-fitting, tunic length spandex jackets over yoga pants? And pearls, of course.

Tip #4. Competition: Hushed announcer's voiceover:

It's the moment we've all been waiting for—Olympic Mothering as current champions vie for the gold. Today's distinguished panel of judges includes USA's Betty Draper, UK's Queen Elizabeth, and HELL's Saddam Hussein (who only agreed to appear because of a faulty translation of the phrase 'The Battle of All Mothers').

The first contestant is Barb Taub in her breakfast routine. For those viewers unfamiliar with Championship Mothering, in this round contestants perform required moves, and judges issue separate scores for Mona Lisa Smile and Technique. Extra points are awarded if the child involved is a male. However, points will be lost for obscenities, corporal punishment, and visits by social workers.

Barb gets a strong start with the move that bears her name. With the famous Barb Hammerlock, she gets three kids out of bed and dressed for school. Moving smoothly into the required Oatmeal Death Spiral, Barb places each child in front of a steaming bowl. It looks like a perfect move. But wait! In the follow-through whining and gagging, she wobbles, and exchanges the oatmeal for toaster pastries.

But oatmeal is one of the most difficult mothering moves, so this may not cost her too much. Like a champion, she heads straight into the school lunches. This is a tricky move—she can lose points both if the lunches are not nutritious and if they are not eaten. But I think she's nailed it with this one! Chocolate cupcakes laced with ground-up vitamins and antibiotics! The crowd goes wild!

Be with us tomorrow for the short routines in which contestants potty-train two-year-olds while simultaneously enrolling them in Harvard Medical School. And let's cheer Barb on as she attempts to bring home a gold medal. Or at least a dryer.

❖ ❖ ❖

Chapter 5: Penis Envy Or The Revenge Of Your Sixth-Grade Science Teacher

"To feel envy is human, to savor schadenfreude is devilish." —Arthur Schopenhauer, <u>On Human Nature</u>

Lao Tzu said, *"Manifest plainness, Embrace simplicity, Reduce selfishness, Have few desires."*

Obviously, old Lao Tzu was never a parent. And if he was a parent, he wasn't the Mom in charge of Lao Junior's science fair project. As women, we know about envy. Penis envy? Oh please, that's for amateurs. Those of us who've turned envy into Olympic-level competition (aka: mothers) know there are few public forums better suited to pro-level envy than their child's science fair project expo night.

By the time we've accepted that our spawn will probably not be flashing that Superbowl ring or supermodel contract, we're pretty much into laser-focused envy in areas where we can actually have some effect. Forget curing cancer or promoting world peace. World-class maternal envy focuses on whether other women's children will do better on their SATs, snag admission to CalTech or MIT, and generate billions on their first IPO while our child is still living in our basement, working in a comic book store, and trying to find himself. This usually develops well before all children in question have hit kindergarten, so by the time they're called on to produce science fair projects, we mothers have had several years to ~~obsess~~ ~~terrify~~ mentor our children. (And no, Mr. Freud—we seldom waste our finely-honed ninja envy skills on things that would just be handy to have along on a picnic.)

I was thinking about this because a friend sent me one of those articles about genius kids whose science fair projects involved using household items to cure the common cold, produce cold fusion, or get rid of garden pests and Justin Bieber. So I dug out the following column I wrote for the *Champaign Urbana News Gazette* (way the hell long ago).

❖ ❖ ❖

Science Fair and the Attraction of Opposites

Opposites don't just attract. They marry, reproduce, and give their in-laws something to blame the children's faults on. For example, marriages are often made up of Savers and Wasters. In ours, Waster (me) takes long hot showers while Saver (Hub) sneaks down to the water heater and lowers the water temperature. He considers any articles unused in the last two weeks the rightful property of Goodwill while I don't notice clutter unless it starts to move around and ask for seconds at dinner.

I bring light to the house and joy to the hearts of power company stockholders while he questions empty rooms. "Who left this light on?" In the interest of efficiency, in fact, he often turns off the lights in occupied rooms, on the general theory that eventually the rooms will be empty. He told the emergency room physician who was stitching him up (and anyone else who asked) that I had split his head open because he was saving energy. What he neglected to mention was that my weapon of choice was the closet door I'd left ajar, and which he ran into face first in the dark.

I've been giving the attraction of opposite forces a lot of thought lately. Those of you without school-age children are saying to yourselves, "Barb doesn't have enough to do. She needs a hobby, like spinning dryer lint or seeking the Democratic nomination for president." But parents with school-age children are saying, "Must be Science Fair season again."

If you're new to competitive Science Fair parenting at the pro level, you may need a few tips. Have you found yourself saying, "My kid didn't even get honorable mention at Science Fair? But... we had it all. Styrofoam volcano, electronic buzzers, grow lights, rodents... Now how is she supposed to get into MIT?" You definitely need to check out the following tips (or just redo your basement where, clearly, your kid will be residing for the remainder of your natural life).

The most important thing to realize about a science fair is that it has absolutely nothing to do with science. If it did, it would involve actual scientists, instead of parents whose last documented science fact was absorbed in seventh grade biology class when they discovered that the disturbingly long earthworms they were dissecting would fit neatly through the door holes in someone's locker. Science fairs are actually a promotional gimmick dreamed up by the rodent and little electronic buzzer industries. This is why 89.9% of all science fair projects involve rodents, little electronic buzzers, or rodents ringing little electronic buzzers. (The other 10.1% involves volcanoes, of course.)

[EXAMPLE OF WINNING SCIENCE FAIR EXPERIMENT: Rodent pushes little electronic buzzer in maze, triggering volcano.]

The 10-year-old mentioned casually last weekend that her science fair project was due on Wednesday. "But don't worry," she assured me. "I have the experiment all planned. I'm going to investigate whether my rodent can see color by having her run a maze involving little colored lights leading to a peanut-reward." If the rodent made it, we'd all stand around and ring little electronic buzzers.

It was a great idea, but we ran into two problems. The first problem was that every little electronic buzzer in a three-state region had been snapped up by her classmates. (These buzzer-buyers have a great future as pre-meds who check out ALL the library copies of assigned class-readings and keep them until after finals.) The second problem was that our only resident rodent is a senior citizen hamster who tends to bite people on the fleshy part of the nose if she's feeling crotchety. Asking our geriatric rodent to run the maze seemed like pulling Grandma out of the rest home and sending her to work at Walmart. The only other rodents we could think of who might be willing to brave the bright lights for peanuts were all off campaigning for the off-year primaries.

Which brings us back to the theory of the attraction of opposite forces. *[See what I did there? I'm a professional writer, though, so don't try this at home kids.]* My children were trying to explain to me how the crystal radio they built could work without batteries. It seemed to have something to do with magnets being attracted to rock music radio waves. I suggested that if they could explain it to a science-impaired person like me, it might pass at science fair.

We started with the basics. My daughter showed me how you can make your own compass by sticking a needle through a bead of styrofoam, rubbing it against a magnet and floating it in a bowl of water. I understood this phenomenon perfectly. It's caused by magic. After that, she lost me in technical details of transformers, coils, and radio transmitters. The final results were so impressive that I didn't even bring up nitpicking little details like whether I'd get back the stereo's transformer or the starting coil from my car's engine. (After all, we have a crystal radio and an excellent bus system.)

But something still seemed to be missing. Maybe if she added a rodent holding a little electronic buzzer?

♦ ♦ ♦

Chapter 6: Etiquette Lessons For Attila The Hun

"Schadenfreude: *the experience of pleasure, joy, or self-satisfaction that comes from learning of or witnessing the troubles, failures, or humiliation of another."—<u>Wikipedia</u>*

We were celebrating my birthday last week at a lovely London restaurant, and my toddler grandchild could not believe her luck when the waitress set a plate with a hamburger and french fries in front of her. She beamed at her new best friend, and confided the numbers one-to-ten in English *and* Spanish. (Minus the number six, of course, because for reasons we don't quite understand, that number is dead to her. It must never be mentioned.)

The beginning of this beautiful friendship was cut short, however, when the waitress came back later and took her plate away. The baby fixed her with a glare so terrible paint cracked on the wall behind her. Grown men turned white and headed for the bar, while a nearby dog hid under a table. The focussed power of the stink-eye leveled on our server was so alarming, the accompanying wail so ear-piercing, that the plate-thief stumbled back to the kitchen for safety. While my kids tried to apologize, I thought about the process of civilizing small children—and the sheer joy of knowing it's their problem now. As one friend commented, "Revenge is a dish best served in grandchildren-sized portions."

My husband learned etiquette at dancing class, where he acquired such life skills as the fox trot, cutting in, and not wearing white socks.

I learned etiquette from Our Lady of Plaid High School's lecture series: "Young Ladies Shouldn't____"

- sing along with the chorus to Country Joe's war protest—"*Give me an*

F, give me a U, [etc]"—during the bishop's annual school visit.

- appear in public with minimal skirts, maximal makeup, or unrelated men with facial hair.

- refuse a religious vocation to convent life from the Holy Spirit. *(I can only attribute the nun's enthusiasm for this last lecture to their belief in miracles.)*

I remember when our first male teacher—a graduate student from Berkeley trying to maintain his draft exemption—arrived to sub for Sister Mary History because she had a Religious Crisis during third period. Sister had brought us down to the library to do some research, and Carol Dougherty discovered she could use her purse mirror to focus a beam of light on the dove in the mosaic tile floor. Twenty-three mirror beams were making the dove do tricks when Sister noticed. Informing us that the Holy Spirit was making a Third Period History visitation, she made us get down on our knees to pray for world peace and a vocation to religious life. When the bell rang, she wouldn't let us leave until Sister Mary Office came down to find out what was going on. Sister Mary History got a long...*long* rest, and we got the "Young Ladies Shouldn't Give Elderly Nuns Nervous Breakdowns" lecture, along with a new (male) teacher.

The next day our new history teacher, Mr. Martin, wrote his name on the board and turned to face us. He grew pale, broke out in a sweat, and bolted from the room. A few minutes later, Sister Mary Office gave us the "Young Ladies With Uniform Skirts Rolled Up Into Micro-Minis Shouldn't Straddle Their Desks" lecture. (Mr. Martin volunteered for active duty in Viet Nam soon after, and Sister Mary Office taught Third Period History for the rest of the year. I didn't learn much about the ancient world, but I did learn the correct filing rules for tricky bits like M/Mc/Mac...)

Then the Hub and I got married, squeaked through wedding etiquette land mines, and thought we were home free. When our first child was potty trained, we figured our job as her parents was pretty much completed. Oh sure, we'd spend a few more years together, maybe contribute to a couple of orthodontists' or orthopedic surgeons' retirement funds. But basically, we assumed that our next big parental task was going to be be dropping said child off at her college dormitory.

What we soon realized is that between these two events comes the job of civilizing a little being with less appreciation for the social niceties than Attila the Hun. (If only I had a dollar for every time I said, "No, you can't have your own flamethrower. It's rude to torch the neighbors, even if they don't want to play your way.")

While I tackled the easy issues like social acceptability of weapons of mass destruction, body noises, and precision spitting, my husband was made for sterner stuff. He sat the kids down to teach them restaurant etiquette. This is a job for a strong man because although our kids couldn't cut up their own meat yet, they were masters at finding parental logic-loopholes through cross-examinations that would make Clarence Darrow look like an amateur.

NAPKINS:

Dad: "Unfold your napkin and keep it on your lap."

Child#1: "What if you put something in your mouth that tastes so terrible you know if you swallow it you'll throw up so you want to spit it into your napkin but your napkin fell on the floor and the dog ate it?"

Dad: "Uh…"

NICETIES

Dad: "You should always talk to the person sitting on each side of you."

Child#2: "What if it's someone gross and disgusting like (insert name of any boy in the entire universe) and when I say something nice he punches me? Or what if he passes me the creamed rutabagas even though I've said 187 times what will happen if I so much as smell the creamed rutabagas? Or what if he's eating his creamed rutabagas when suddenly he throws up in them?"

Dad: "Uh…"

NOSES:

Dad: "If you have to sneeze or blow, use a tissue, not your napkin."

Child#3: "What if I don't have a tissue and it's an emergency blow?"

Dad: "So okay, use your napkin."

Child#3: "What if I sneeze so fast I can't even get my napkin and what's in my mouth goes all over the dress of the person at the next table and I can't wipe it up because I still have that napkin Child#1 spit something disgusting into?"

Dad: "Uh…"

REVIEW OF DAD'S ETIQUETTE LESSONS

Child#1: "If the person across from you spits watermelon seeds at you, don't spit them back. They might have his germs on them, so use your own seeds."

Child#2: "Don't eat creamed rutabagas if you're wearing white socks."

Child#3: "Keep your knees together if you've spit something into your napkin."

Dad: "Uh…"

Mom: "We can't wait until you have your own children."

❖ ❖ ❖

Chapter 7: Top Ten Things My Father Taught Me

Today is the first Father's Day without my dad, and I've been thinking of some of the things he taught me. Here's a quick list of the top ten:

Ten: <u>Take care of your shoes.</u> With ten kids, shoe leather represented a significant investment for my parents. My father had a shoe shine box, and made sure we all knew how to polish our (and his!) shoes. I can still remember the heady fumes of Kiwi brand shoe polish with its little open/shut key on the side, and how astonished my college roomies were when they saw me applying ox-blood red (the ultimate in classy shine) to the one pair of boots I had for all four years.

Nine: <u>Look it up.</u> Never use one little word when a big one (or two) will do. If we didn't know the answer, that's what the *Funk & Wagnalls New World Encyclopedia* that we bought one volume at a time from trading stamps at the grocery store was for. (We just had to hope the answer wasn't in volume St-Te because we somehow got two of the preceding volumes instead.) By the end of an average family dinner, multiple volumes would be open on the table.

Eight: <u>"Vacation" is a matter of semantics.</u> Sure, some of his colleagues took their families on ski vacations and trips to Europe. My father crammed kids into the Vomit-Comet and took us to the drive-in for mini rootbeer floats. Every few years there would be a road trip from California to visit the relatives back east. We'd pull into a KOA campground each night, amazing nearby campers with the speed at which we set up tents. What they didn't realize was that nobody got to go to the bathroom until that was done. Thanks to those road trips, my siblings and I have great memories and strong bladder control.

Seven: <u>You say "cheap" like it's a bad thing.</u> The winner is the one who finds the gas station where Regular is 2-cents cheaper. Even if you had to spend that much to drive there. This was so ingrained that I was shocked when a date handed me a dollar and begged me to go to the nearest gas station, just because I'd been cruising on fumes looking for the best deal. I took the dollar and dumped the date.

Six: <u>Car maintenance.</u> His daughters had to be able to change a tire, check our oil and water, use (and always carry) battery cables, drive a manual transmission, and hang out in the garage with him while my father fixed everything else on our cars. On TV, Dads would come into their TV-daughters' bedrooms (the ones with the princess light-up phones, frilly curtains, and matching canopy beds that they didn't have to share with two other sisters) and give poignant, valuable life lessons. In our house, we handed our father the wrench, and sat in the front seat to push the brake/gas pedal/ clutch as requested. So far, none of us has ended up an ax-murderer.

Five: <u>There is always plenty of food and room for family.</u> If you rang our doorbell at dinner time and you were a cousin, knew a cousin, or correctly guessed the partial name of a cousin, you were brought in, another plate was jammed into the dozen already set up, two kids were moved over to the stools next to the kitchen island, and you got the first serving of pot roast. Meanwhile, two or three kids were evicted from the "guest" room and you were urged to stay the night. At least.

Four: <u>If you don't vote, you don't get to complain.</u> *"News Hour"* was a sacred ritual, ammunition and fodder for the sixty+-year Republican vs Democrat debate in which my father and my mother never missed the opportunity to cancel each other's vote.

Three: <u>Go to college.</u> People used to ask how he got all ten kids to go to college. The answer was simple: we all thought our only choices were go to college or go to Notre Dame. Some people have dead animal heads or fish as trophies, but my father's proudest souvenirs from his victories over forty-plus years of tuition payments were displayed in his case containing mugs from each of our colleges.

Two: <u>Stop and help.</u> If I was driving home late at night and I saw a couple of cars pulled over, one with the hood up, I could almost guarantee that the second car would be my father's. It never occurred to him to wait for someone to ask for help. On one of our road trips, our trailer was demolished when we were caught in the side winds of a passing tornado. All of us and what belongings we could salvage were crammed into the car, piled literally up to the roof. We'd been driving across the desert for hours and hadn't seen a single car in any direction when we passed a car pulled off the road. Of course my father stopped and offered to help. When he couldn't get their car started, he offered the young couple a ride. They looked at our car in disbelief and told him they would wait for the next car. To the end of his life, my father worried about what became of them.

And the Number One thing I learned from my father? <u>What to leave behind.</u> Like most parents, my father worried about leaving an estate for his children. But his devotion to our education ensured that we'd have the tools to build wonderful lives for ourselves. And his legacy of how to be the best possible person, parent, and friend did far more to guarantee a good life for his children than the material possessions he left behind.

❖ ❖ ❖

Chapter 8: Top 10 Reasons Not To Be My Father

Ten was an important number to my father—the number of kids he had to send to college, the (minimum) number of years to keep each car, the number of miles out of his way he'd go to save 2-cents on a gallon of gas... So it seems only fitting to list the ten top worst reasons to be my father.

10. Gift-Aversion: Some things in life are easy to do: gush over babies, write blogs, cure cancer. Some are harder: get a bikini-wax, reform the tax structure, buy my father a present. With ten kids, he got a LOT of birthday/Christmas/Father's Day presents. It's not that he didn't appreciate what we gave him. "This (wallet/tie/shirt/belt) is *just* what I needed," he would thank us. Then he'd repackage the wallet/tie/shirt/belt and put it away to marinate in his drawer for a few years. *[Full disclosure: there may have been a few occasions when we re-wrapped the wallet/tie/shirt/belt offerings and re-gifted them. To him. Again. Luckily, each time they were JUST what he needed.]*

9. 40 Years of College Tuition: I've heard people ask, "How did your parents get all ten children to go to college?" The answer was simple: we all thought the only choice we had in the matter was whether to just go to college or to go to Notre Dame. For several generations, so many in my father's family went to Notre Dame that I was an adult before I realized there are some births, weddings, or funerals where they *don't* play the *Notre Dame Fight Song*.

8. Doing-It-Yourself: My father was the ultimate home handyman. Of course this was before *This Old House* told us to use the right tool for every job. Maybe because he didn't have This Old Toolshed the size of Milwaukee, my father fixed everything that ever went wrong in our house with a hammer, a wrench, or a needle-nosed pliers. For really tough jobs—he holds the world's record for

diapers extracted from toilet guts—he also used a coat hanger.

7. Applied Engineering: Perhaps it was his engineering training which allowed my father to see how simple solutions (usually involving coat hangers) can be adapted to any situation. My mother claimed it explained her gray hair when she told about looking up to the roof of their two-story house to see my father hanging upside down from the gutters with a can of paint swinging gaily from a coat hanger beside him. Actually, he survived this method better than the one he used when he decided to touch up the second floor siding while the rest of the family packed for a family trip. Perhaps feeling that scaffolding was only for people without enough life insurance, he stacked his ladder on top of the picnic table. Most people who fall 2 ½ stories go to an emergency room. Our family went to Sacramento. His nose, he insisted, always had that big lump in the middle. The two black eyes were a nice touch too—it was like touring with a giant panda, only they have smaller snouts.

6. Brake Conservation: Every couple of years, my father would load us into the Vomit-Comet**, and head back east to visit relatives.

> **[So named because he didn't believe in "wearing out" the brakes by using them on twisting mountain roads, and also–following that time my brother took a nose dive from the car as it conserved brakes on the road above Lake Tahoe–windows were firmly shut at all times. Despite his cigar.]*

One year, he decided to save on motel rooms by towing a little pop-up camper. Neighboring campers were so impressed when kids boiled from our arriving car and raced to set up the camper and tent. What those strangers didn't know was that nobody got to go to the bathroom until it was done.

Alas, because of another of his little economies (car radios were an expensive 'option' for rich people), we missed the report of the upcoming tornado. The car was dragged across several lanes of freeway by the pop-up camper, which finally flipped over and smashed. When the highway patrol arrived, they were stopped in their tracks by the scale of the carnage—sleeping bags, toys, and children's clothing mixed with unidentifiable bloody globs of what looked like hamburger. Luckily, it WAS hamburger: fifty pounds that was meant to get us across the country. Abandoning the trailer, my father grimly loaded all of us back into the Vomit Comet, stacked what clothing he could salvage into the cracks, and set off across the desert.

We'd been driving for hours without passing a car in either direction when we saw a young couple whose little VW had broken down in the middle of the desert. My father stopped and offered a lift. Looking at the station wagon packed to the roof with children surrounded by bloody clothing, they decided to wait another day—maybe two—until another car came by. I'm guessing they remained childless.

<u>5. No Kissing</u>: I don't come from a physically affectionate family. When our church added the Kiss of Peace, I thought my father would start his own church, but he contented himself with locking his arms across his chest and glaring indignantly at approaching members of the congregation. So to us kids, the approach of visiting relatives meant one thing—enforced embraces to be avoided at all costs.

To distract ourselves from his driving, we older kids would spend cross-country trips laying out a military campaign which involved sending in a suicide-squad of the younger kids to brave the first wave of relatives' affection while we attempted kiss-evasive flanking maneuvers. It took 2,000 miles of coaching and almost got us all put up for adoption, but our greatest triumph was the year we taught the baby to respond to kisses with, "Well. I have *never* in my whole life been so em-*BARE*-assed."

<u>4. Dinner-Table Etiquette</u>: Remember gloriously doomed battles like the Alamo, the Charge of the Light Brigade, the Battle of the Little Bighorn, my father's efforts to get a word in edgewise amongst his eight daughters' conversation? What does history tell us of the many who stood bravely against overwhelming odds?

History: "They were dead meat."

With eight daughters, my outnumbered father shifted uncomfortably during dinner discussions between those of us whose developing physical endowments split us into the Haves and Have-Nots. He insisted that we refer to bras as 'articles', but I don't think that helped much.

Sister #1: "Did you hear about the girls up at Berkeley who are burning their articles?"

Sister #2: "Without their miracle-articles, won't they jiggle?"

Sister #3: I'd love to have enough to jiggle. I could replace my articles with band-aids and nobody could tell the difference."

Sister #4: "You're lucky. At least you won't get all saggy when you get old, like thirty."

Sister #5: "And have you seen the articles you have to wear when you get pregnant? They could hold basketballs…"

Father: "I'll be eating dinner in the garage until the baby leaves for college…"

<u>3. Scary Weddings:</u> Ten children. Eight of them daughters. As we grew, my father frequently mentioned his willingness to supply ladders to any offspring

who would consider eloping. But I'd seen his ladders, usually balanced on top of the picnic table. So I was the first sister to commit an actual wedding. Before the wedding I made a list of each person's tasks in the three weeks before the event.

- ME: 1. Choose wedding dress for mother to veto. 2. Be on time for the ceremony.

- HUSBAND-2-BE: 1. Finish PhD dissertation so he'll have a job. 2. Be on time for the ceremony. 3. Borrow a tie from my father. 4. Actually wear it.

- MY MOTHER: 1. Type his dissertation so he'll have a job. 2. Bake wedding cake, grow flowers, cook all the food, send out the invitations, find the minister, arrange the ceremony, decorate the house and yard, reserve hotel rooms for his family, plan and host reception. 3. Veto the wedding dress I got at that perfectly nice thrift shop, take my younger sister out to try on dresses, buy another dress, make a veil.

- MY FATHER: 1. Fix the car even if it's not broken. 2. Worry. 3. Cry at ceremony.

My father pretended to be fixing the car until a few days before the wedding. He had to come out from under the car to pick up my uncle, an Air Force chaplain and the only one who would agree to marry us on such short notice. They returned to find the entire household proofreading the dissertation.

Uncle: "Let's discuss the sanctity of holy matrimony. Shouldn't that comma on page 74 be a period?"

Husband-2-Be: "If this dissertation isn't finished, I'm not getting married."

Me: "*Sob!*"

Father: "If anyone needs me, I'll be under the car."

My uncle's sermon at the ceremony the next day was, "Marriage is like a dissertation." My father cried. (Probably at the thought of my six younger, as-yet-unmarried sisters...)

2. Baby Terrorizing: One of my father's favorite ways of demonstrating his love and devotion to his grandchildren was to sneak up on them and yell "BOO!" Sadly, none of his grandchildren was ever enamored of this form of attention, although I have noticed that all grew up to fearlessly navigate the California freeway system.

And the number one reason not to be my father?

1. I never told him that he was the greatest father ever.

❖ ❖ ❖

Chapter 9: In Times Of Trouble, Parents Reached For Pink Stuff

I was talking to my daughter and she mentioned that the days of pouring antibiotics into kids at the first sniffle are over. Today's parents have my sympathy. Here's how we did it back then...

People often ask me if the things I write about really happened. The sad truth is these columns aren't fiction: this is my life. Of course, everything doesn't happen at once. Well, actually my kids are on antibiotics right now, but not the same ones.

They all used to take the same medicine for their ear infections. In the interests of efficiency, each child got a new infection ten days after finishing up their last prescription of Pink Stuff. (Feeding your children Pink Stuff, an antibiotic made from powdered platinum, is only slightly more expensive than mounting your own space program.)My own kids, who think antibiotics are one of the basic food groups, have consumed enough Pink Stuff to send the children of several Pharmaceuticals-R-Us executives through Ivy League colleges. But I'm not complaining: I like diseases that can be cured by Pink Stuff. In fact, strep throat is my favorite illness—24 hours of Pink Stuff, the B-52 of antibiotics, and the kids are back in school where they belong.

Rx: Powered Platinum (3x/day until wallet is empty)

A few years ago, my husband had to make a business trip to another continent, but I wasn't worried about handling things without him. Our house was for sale, the dog had developed a mysterious compulsion to perform unnatural acts involving the cow manure in the pasture behind our house, and all three kids were on Pink Stuff—in other words, things were pretty normal.

There is a clause in my wifehood contract which states that in such circumstances, I (the wife of the first part) shall be permitted to complain to him (the husband of the last possible part) that mothers never have conventions involving beaches on foreign coasts. Such complaints are not to exceed the number of times I draw breath, up to and including the moment said husband boards his plane.

I have added a rider which states said husband must also say to me at least once, "I wish you could go to my conference being held at a resort in an exotic foreign country and I could stay here with the kids." If he chokes on the words, he has to start over. My husband, however, is a professional. He managed to look sad as he said how much he would miss us, and (in a remarkable demonstration of iron-willed self-control) avoided sprinting up the ramp to his plane.

By the next morning, my two-year-old son had developed an all-body rash. Our pediatrician was baffled. Exhaustive allergy testing had earlier revealed the two-year-old was not allergic to anything except air, food, plants, animals, and of course his siblings. Within hours, his joints were swollen to the size of softballs, and the rash had colonized his entire skin surface. His sisters were very impressed.

The pediatrician referred us to the allergist over in Roanoke, who asked if I could bring him immediately. Since this only meant loading three sick kids and a dog into a non-air-conditioned car for a ninety-minute drive on Virginia mountain roads in 95-degree weather, I said we'd be right over. About halfway there, I noticed two things. The first was my son gasping for breath. The second was the smoke pouring from under the hood of my ancient Volvo wagon.

I did what anybody with my extensive knowledge of car maintenance and repair would have done: ignored the smoke and drove on.

By the time I made it into Roanoke, I had the freeway to myself. A few drivers assumed I just hadn't noticed the smoke cheerily steaming from my engine. Bravely, they pulled up alongside, honking and pointing frantically at the hood. Nodding and smiling like the Queen of Valium, I waved them on—nothing to worry about, it always does this…

My son only had to spend one day in the hospital, which none of us minded because it was air-conditioned. Unfortunately, the car also survived and was repaired by the time he was ready to go home.

But the real tragedy was that the cause of all his trouble was Pink Stuff. Now when he gets an ear-infection on his ten-day cycle, we have to use inferior scud-antibiotics instead of sending in the carpet-bombing Pink Stuff.

The rest of my husband's absence passed smoothly. (No, we don't need to go into how I gave myself a concussion when I decided to repaint the kitchen cabinets. It could happen to anybody. Luckily, I recovered before he got back and didn't even need any Pink Stuff.)

❖ ❖ ❖

Chapter 10: How To Raise A Son. Or Not...

When he was two, we tried to block our son's view of any appliances we were using. Just to slow him down. That was also the year the police came to the door, responding to "our" 911 call. We heard toddler giggling from his crib, where he was holed up with the portable phone.

When he was three, we had to replace the microwave after he vaporized a bunch of bananas. (And who can forget the time he backed the car into traffic?)

When he was four, I came home to find that not one but three outlets in the kitchen were now smoking black holes. (His father claims he didn't hear a thing.)

When he was six, he wrote a letter (which I mailed) to the Pentagon demanding an explanation for the rule that six-year-olds couldn't have their own flamethrowers. Wisely, the Pentagon declined to answer.

When he was eight, I decided TV wasn't a good influence, so I got rid of the cable and the antenna. He built a system to "borrow" the neighbor's signal, which he and his sisters trotted out every time I left the house.

To everyone's astonishment, he's lived long enough to become a (reasonably) responsible dues-paying member of society. Who knew?

But some things never change, as his recent Mother's Day Card clearly indicates...

Dear Mama:

REASONS WHY YOU WERE THE BEST MOTHER AN EVIL GENIUS COULD HOPE FOR

1. You found it cute and endearing when I assembled suspicious-looking objects out of cardboard and old electronics.

2. You bought me a book with the Evil Overlord List in it.

3. Instead of sending me to summer camp, you bought me robotics lessons.

4. You documented my early life in a humor column, which will be a real time-saver while explaining my villainous backstory and/or those first meetings with future therapists.

5. You bought me a power-tool set, woodburning pen, and something called a "Slimy Creepy Crawly Oven" and allowed me to use them unsupervised.

6. When frustrated with the noises (and okay, the smells) my electronics made, you only sabotaged them a little, providing me with many opportunities to learn about electrical repair and rewiring.

HAPPY MOTHER'S DAY!

◆ ◆ ◆

Chapter 11: A Mother's Day (CAUTIONARY) Fairy Tale

Once upon a time (and we're talking LONG time), there was a poor Mom named CinderBarb, who married her academic-gypsy prince. They moved to Illinois, where CinderBarb began to look for a castle. As she soon learned, in central Illinois, castle basements came in two forms—finished (floors) and unfinished (not so much). Unfinished basements had exposed plumbing and wiring, dirt (or, in some newer castles, cement) floors, and regular floods. Finished basements had plumbing and wiring covered with d ark faux-wood paneling, cement floors with shag carpeting, and regular floods.

From her fairy godRealtor, CinderBarb learned that when her children are small, they are supposed to say, "Let's play happily all winter down in the sub-arctic unfinished basement even though it's basically the place that you scream to the blonde teen in the slasher movie to stay out of. Unless she has to do the laundry, of course." Then when they become teenagers, their parents bring on the paneling, shag carpet, and the stereo, and the kids will say, "Let's go down into our neat basement and play some swell board games instead of drag racing down University Avenue, drinking beer in the parking lot, and scoring drugs from students at the U."

So CinderBarb bought Entropy House (unfinished basement) where she was forced by her wicked step-socioeconomic status to slave from dawn to dusk and where nature, not to mention the dog, abhorred a vacuum. At Entropy House, CinderBarb's prince was always asking when *we* [can't you just see those air-quotes?] are going to finish moving into our house. But somehow in their whole whirlwind home-by-midnight-with-a-PhD courtship, CinderBarb never got around to mentioning her genetic impairment. Sadly, she was born with a congenital Martha Stewart deficiency. Her only coping mechanism when moving to a new castle is to line up the furniture around the walls and hang her two pictures in existing nail-holes in hopes the previous tenants had better decorating skills. She leaves the actual redecorating until they put the castle on the market and the fairy godRealtor hints that while it's all very well for lower forms of life like them (Sellers), real humans (Buyers) are going to require roofs and carpeting installed in the current century.

But even CinderBarb had to admit that having a family room decorated in early U-Schlep boxes might not be the Better Castles & Gardens effect she's after. She lacked the nerve to actually look inside the boxes, many of which had followed them, unopened, through the last several castles. Movers cryptically labelled some of the U-Schleps with phrases like "*MB—misc.sn.pit.*" While this might mean "Master Bedroom—miscellaneous snapshots and pictures," CinderBarb couldn't shake the suspicion they actually contained a variety of snake pits belonging to somebody with the initials "M.B."

So one day she channelled Mary Poppins: "Let us all clean out the basement and move these boxes down there. There will be fun and much pizza." As with most of her worst ideas, CinderBarb refused to listen to the voice of reason— which in Entropy House was rarely heard above the din anyway—as she deployed her troops into the depths.

At first it wasn't too bad. The four-year-old, King of Boxes & Junk, began to pile up his cardboard treasures while his sisters gathered about 375 stuffed animals nobody had played with in years. If ever. Carried away by her excitement at catching a glimpse of the actual basement floor, CinderBarb uttered the word that broke the magic spell: "trash". The King threw himself across Mt. Cardboard screaming, "NO CinderMom, you can't throw out that box. It's my airplane." She reached for another box. "Not that one either. It's my duck house. In case I get a duck." She pointed to a little one in the back. "Nope. Spaceship."

CinderBarb pondered the immortal words of W.C. Fields. "If at first you don't succeed try again. Then give up. No use being a damned fool about it." When the King's back was turned, she bravely threw out an old waffle box.

Meanwhile, his sisters held a wake for their stuffed animals. Somehow they knew CinderBarb couldn't get rid of anything with an obituary. "This is Fluffy/Bluey/Mary/Dolly/Baby/etc. I got her from Grandmom/Aunt Tilly/Uncle Toots and I LOVE her. If you throw her out, I'm going to tell them and they'll probably get me TWO more. Big ones."

Bowing to the inevitable, she remortgaged the castle, purchasing thirty-seven miles of shelving to hold all of the King's junk, stuffed animals, boxes of books, and toys from upstairs. It took her family the better part of a week to haul it all upstairs again. "My next castle," vowed CinderBarb, "...will have a magic attic where these boxes can live happily ever after."

Chapter 12: Hairy Scary

I came in one day to find the kitchen phone amputated from its cord. Although I tried emergency phone first-aid, it was too late: our family phone had gone to that big exchange in the sky where all receivers are gently cradled and all calls are from lovers, mothers, and the Publishers' Clearinghouse Sweepstakes.

In reconstructing the crime, I eliminated the Hub as a suspect. Although I find it efficient to pin all disasters on him, even I had to admit the only phone calls he or I get are from life insurance salespersons congratulating us on the birth of our latest child and asking if we have reformulated our estate planning needs to reflect our new responsibilities. We usually tell them our estate plan is to spend every penny faster than we make it and then retire to live off our kids. (If that doesn't work, we hand the phone to the baby and tell her the nice man wants to hear the song of her people.)

I also eliminated the eight-year-old. Not only is he the only one who knows how to use the memory dial, but if he had been behind the phone's untimely demise, I'm sure he would have performed an autopsy as well.

Of course, those of you with daughters are saying to yourselves, "I'll bet there's a long-haired teenage girl involved." And you'd be right. Engrossed in imparting to her friend the details of all that had befallen since they'd parted at school 23 minutes earlier, my daughter failed to notice when her hair mated with the coils of the phone cord, which then required emergency separation surgery (the phone cord, not her hair).

Personally, I don't like hair. The way I see it, if God meant us to have long hair, She wouldn't have given us scissors or Vidal Sassoon. But when I hint to my daughter that she consider trimming her hair before it gets stepped on, she acts like I'm suggesting shortening her legs or cropping her ears so she'll win Best of Show.

So I decided to do what any normal, hair-averse mother would do. I tried to scare her into getting a haircut. "Did I ever tell you about your aunt and the cookies?"

She looked apprehensive and started edging toward the door, so I spoke quickly:

Once upon a time before they invented cholesterol, your aunt decided to make cookies. Now, Grandmother's mixer was not for the faint-hearted cook. She had one of those industrial-strength, 1950s cast-iron MixMasters with removable implements which could juice a turkey or sausage large farm animals in moments.

Mother forbid us to even look in its direction when she wasn't home, implying that it would have liked nothing better than to remove a few of our fingers just for practice. Nevertheless, one day while Mother was out, chocolate chip cookies started calling my sister's name. (In my family, there is an inherited genetic defect which causes many of us to be born imprinted with the racial memory of chocolate chip cookie and brownie recipes. When they call us, we are helpless to resist.)

Soon she had mixed all the cookie ingredients and was just adding the chocolate chips when one of her long braids strayed over the bowl and the mixer went on the offensive. The next thing she knew, her hair had been whipped into the beaters and it took all her strength to keep her ear from being juiced. She screamed for assistance, but it took the siblings who came running a few minutes to recover from the sight of their sister with her entire head in a bowl of cookie dough.

Finally, the mixer was unplugged and the braid extricated from the dough. But there was one more problem. If our mother discovered that not only had the mixer had been used, but also that all the dough wasted, we would probably not get a cookie fix again that century. So by the time Mother got home, my sister's hair had been washed, and the remaining batter had been baked into cookies.

My father was pleased and touched that, for once, we saved the entire batch of cookies just for him.

"So," I concluded. "Does this story make you want to get your hair cut?"

"Not really," answered my daughter. "But now I really want a cookie. At least now I know why I instinctively know the exact Toll House recipe."

When threats fail, it is time to remind myself that I'm the grownup here. Luckily, over a decade of parenting experience has prepared me to play the one card that never fails. "Cut your hair and I'll take you to Disneyland."

◆ ◆ ◆

Chapter 13: How To Embarrass Your Child

I went to a socially-impaired university. It was a time of revolution and experimentation with sex, drugs, music among kids: in other words, it was just like today. But the University of Chicago's claim to "The Life of the Mind" reassured parents. Fathers of teenage daughters thought the mind was a lot safer place to live than where they remembered spending their college years, "The Life of the Party".

We had friends from other colleges who had social lives and arrest records, so we knew what we were missing. And it wasn't as though we didn't try. We'd stay up all night or even close out the college's only bar, Jimmy's, discussing the eternal questions:

- Is there a God?
- How do you get rid of roaches?
- Who's got the $10 for the muggers on the way home?
- How can I make the world more fair?
- Why am I here?

I was lucky. I didn't get mugged (that often); the stitches didn't scar (much); I did graduate (eventually). And, after all these years, I've even answered all the questions:

- There *is* a God and She has a sense of humor. It's the only possible explanation for Chicago politics and for two-year-olds.
- The only way to get rid of roaches is to move out. Or get a divorce.
- You still need $10 for the trip home because the child who has refused to eat for the whole trip will announce that she is going to die from hunger if you don't stop at the Chez Mac's ten minutes from home.

- I don't care if it's not fair: I'm the mother and I say so.
- I am here to embarrass and torture my children.

Amateur parents may be concerned about this last requirement. How could you ever embarrass your children? Don't worry. Not only will you discover just how much fun it is to mess with their little heads, but you won't have to actually do a thing to achieve it. As soon as your child turns ten, there will be a few things about you which they will find embarrassing, such as your car, your appearance, your clothes, your habit of speaking to them in public, your very existence…

After all, if your child didn't have you to complain about, they might have to fall back on other distractions (romantic partners with facial hair or other precociously developed secondary sexual characteristics and/or enticing vices, for example). To avoid this, it is your job to provide as much anguish as possible. To help you, I have consulted with a panel of experts: my daughter's sixth grade class. *(Her teacher should really know by now not to leave the class alone with parent volunteers like me.)* From the students' vast parentally-imposed embarrassment experience, they produced the following (actual) suggestions:

1. While chaperoning your child's school field trips, ask frequently if he needs to use the toilet. If he takes too long, stand outside and yell in, "Honey are you okay? Are you having *that PROBLEM* again?"

2. Whenever her friends are around, tell your child how much you love her. Also, stand up in church and invite everybody to come to her school play.

3. Show your child's baby pictures (especially the naked ones) to his friends. And be sure to let them know that his nickname was "Droopy-Drawers".

4. Surprise your child by buying her a practical, sturdy, tastefully-matched and well-fitting wardrobe. Then give all her baggy shorts and holey t-shirts to the Goodwill.

5. Go to your child's soccer game, even though you know nothing about soccer. Whenever the ball comes near her, yell, "Do *that thing* with the ball!" If her coaches aren't mothers, they'll probably appreciate it if you step in and organize practice yourself.

6. Drive your child around in a van or station wagon with at least two carseats and plenty of graham cracker crumbs on the seats. If you are considering a new car, and your teenager is approaching driving age (which they consider to be any time after age twelve), be sure to get one which is large and slow, preferably beige or brown. If you have a

girl, get a very used pickup truck. With a gun rack, of course.

7.   Get a volunteer job at your child's school. Then come into his class and say, "Dear, you forgot to put on clean underwear this morning, so I brought you this fresh pair."

◆ ◆ ◆

Chapter 14: Baking

"What I love about cooking is that after a hard day, there is something comforting about the fact that if you melt butter and add flour and then hot stock, IT WILL GET THICK! It's a sure thing! It's a sure thing in a world where nothing is sure; it has a mathematical certainty in a world where those of us who long for some kind of certainty are forced to settle for crossword puzzles."—Nora Ephron, *Heartburn*, 1983

It was only a matter of time. After planning 4,745 dinners over the years, I stood in front of the refrigerator and admitted the ugly truth. "I've tried, I've really tried. But I just can't think of a thing to make for dinner tonight."

My real problem with menu-planning is that my family is made up of two kinds of eaters, those who'll eat everything (*"This is the best Yak aspic I've ever tasted!"*), and those who'll eat nothing (*"Not fillet mignon AGAIN!"*)

The food section in the newspaper isn't much help. Sure, it keeps Home Economics majors off the streets by letting them write articles like *"Brussels Sprouts Bonanza"* or *"Decorative Okra Carving"*. But just once I'd like to see a recipe which calls for ingredients I actually have in my refrigerator—

> *"Take three geriatric casseroles in which you've been culturing potential cures for cancer, add an industrial strength bottle of ketchup and sixteen opened bottles of pediatric antibiotic."*

The newspapers and magazines often feature some version of the Recipe Gestapo, whose mission is the rehabilitation of politically incorrect recipes:

"Dear Cholesterol Cop: My family loves my casserole made with batter-dipped chicken fried in two pounds of butter and baked in Cream of Onion soup topped with a layer of crusted potato chips. Do we need to modify this recipe?"

Dear Reader: This recipe is fine for those with substantial health and/or life insurance policies. Others may wish to substitute beans for the chicken and pureed tofu for the soup. For increased fiber, add a layer of shredded recycled newspaper printed in soy-based ink. Top with large doses of recreational drugs and your family will never know the difference!"

Luckily, the culinary scientists here at BARB'S have made some important breakthroughs. We began with the question, "How important is sanitation in cooking?" Our research was conducted under the most rigorous conditions possible: my son's preschool classroom, where I agreed to do a cooking project.

I didn't want to pass on any sexist preconceptions, so I announced that we would be making Persons-of-Ginger. (As in the old story, "Run, run as fast as you can, you can't catch me, I'm the Person-of-Ginger.") The boys made dough lumps with long rolls coming out of them. These were Power Ranger Persons-of-Ginger. The girls made dough lumps with long rolls coming out of them. These were Fairy Princess Persons-of-Ginger.

In the final step, the kids sprinkled their creations with colored sugar, chocolate chips, sneezes, and whatever they landed in when they dropped them on the floor. Finally, overcome by the riches before her, one little girl stuffed a handful of sugar sprinkles into her mouth and promptly threw up. *"EEEEWWWW, gross!"* yelled the other chefs. "Can I have the rest of her dough?"

From the fact that the entire class ate their Persons-of-Ginger and lived, we concluded that sanitation in cooking is irrelevant. Further research milestones followed. Who can forget our pathbreaking early discoveries: "It isn't fattening if you eat it standing up" and "Chocolate chip cookie dough has no calories before it's baked".

Now we've met our ultimate challenge: the holiday baking. After years of dedicated research, we are proud to announce the biggest culinary discovery since Pop Tarts: "Desserts baked in months with a "V" or a "D" contain no fat or cholesterol."

You're welcome.

❖ ❖ ❖

Chapter 15: Free Parenting Advice: Worth What You Pay For It

Since I've been writing this column, I have occasionally offered free advice on child-related matters. Apparently some of you don't realize that such advice is worth what you pay for it and, being gluttons for punishment, have asked for more.

QUESTION: Do you have any advice about taking children into restaurants?
ANSWER: Yes. Don't.

QUESTION: But what if you HAVE to take children into restaurants?
ANSWER: Let's analyze what could possibly make you—theoretically an adult capable of life-appropriate decisions as complex as which shoe goes on which foot—take a child into a restaurant:

1.   Insanity.

2.   You're on the road, miles from home and anybody you know.

3.   You've worked 138 hours since last Thursday PLUS the time you spent at the office and you just want a nice, civilized meal that doesn't come on little pierce-film dishes in packages labeled "Le Yuppie Lite". Out of common humanity, we must consider case #3. (In case #1, you can only hope it isn't hereditary and in case #2, who cares?) For those of you who find yourselves in the position of appearing in public with offspring who make Genghis Khan look like a date for Miss Manners, I have a few tips:

   •   The time a child is willing to spend eating in a restaurant is inversely

48

proportional to the cost of the entrée. For example, the same child who spends 3 ½ hours on one bag of french fries at Chez Big Mac will finish eating in 28 seconds flat at Le Vraiment Chic Snail.

- Never eat in a restaurant with ferns. They have obviously been put there to hide something, like the fact the entrees come on little pierce-film dishes. (This advice is part of The Meaning of Life and was given to me by Great Aunt Fanny, a cosmopolitan globe-trotter. If you cannot come up with an Aunt Fanny of your own, you will be reduced to taking advice from some total stranger in a blog.)

- Trust me – your fellow diners WILL NOT be charmed by what your son does every time he gets that diaper off. Do not change the baby's diaper on the table even if the eau d'baby is causing strong men at nearby tables to pass out.

- Unless you don't mind waiting for the rest of your meal until the next shift arrives, it is also not a good idea to hand the offending diaper to your waitperson, especially if the baby is still in it. Remember: even though they pretended to admire your baby, the staff is probably out in the kitchen laying bets on whether the kid looks more like Alfred Hitchcock or a pit bull. The winner gets to spit in your soup.

QUESTION: A colleague will not talk about anything except the respective merits of different brands of disposable diapers. What can we do? ANSWER: This is yet another shocking example of the effects of massive sleep deprivation. Once a regular human, he is now a parent and thus no longer capable of normal conversation. You should help him by taking every opportunity to tell him about your vacations in the south of France, visits to three and four-star restaurants, and the latest concerts or Broadway hit shows you've attended. Also, he would be very interested in your new sports car and high-tech audio equipment and will probably be sympathetic to your concerns about the best tax strategies for your wide-ranging investment portfolio.

[CAUTIONARY NOTE–among very new parents whose metabolism hasn't adjusted to going months at a time without any sleep, the above therapy has been known to result in assault or even homicide charges, for which the author and publishers of this post assume no responsibility.]

QUESTION: My husband wants to get a train set for our son, who is 2 ½ months old. Do you think this is a good idea? ANSWER: Frankly, I'm amazed that your husband has waited this long. A recent scientific study by the Bureau of GSWLOTFGMTUUAVPAS (Government Scientists With Lots of Tax-Funded Grant Money to Use Up And Very Poor Acronym Skills) has indicated that in many cases, news of a woman's positive pregnancy test causes a hormonal reaction in the new father, making him crave model trains. This condition is characterized by changes in his speech patterns, producing sounds such as 'HO Gauge' and 'Lionel'. Although scientists have documented cases of fathers who have been in the basement working on 'the kids' trains since the Korean War, this situation is generally not considered life-threatening unless the victim also starts talking about 'environment accessories' or 'landscape layout'. If this occurs, emergency intervention is necessary. With electric-shock therapy, many of these tragic cases can again become contributing members of society.

❖ ❖ ❖

PART 2: RELATIONSHIPS

◆ ◆ ◆

Chapter 16: Top Ten Reasons Not To Get Married (For Women)

A while ago several of my friends were discussing the number of wedding presents to be purchased this time of year. Somehow (there may have been margaritas involved) the topic turned to things somebody should have mentioned before the I-do's.

My fellow women, many brave margaritas were sacrificed to bring you the cautionary warnings in the following list. If you get married, chances are good your spouse will be a male_____ [*fill in blank from list below. Bonus points if you get all ten.*]**

10. DRIVER: Unless you live in Manhattan or have accumulated buckets of disposable income the old-fashioned way (lottery, inheritance, sneaking onto a city bus that's had an accident so you can claim a back injury), sooner or later you and your husband will find yourselves in the same vehicle without benefit of professional chauffeur. My theory is that there is a boys-only supplemental drivers-ed class girls never see. There (in addition to the cabal hand-signal involving middle fingers) boys learn the sacred tenets of manly driving:

- A man never asks for directions. *GPS/SatNav Corollary*: A man is sure he knows a better route than the satellite directions. He also knows a better route than the cab driver.

- If a woman drives a car belonging to a man who is not suffering from at least two broken limbs (casts are helpful here), other male drivers are required to question his masculinity.

- When a woman is driving, a man knows the importance of pointing out every car, fence, pedestrian, and potential hazard in a three-county region. He also knows she will be grateful. Eventually.

- Under no circumstances will a man make more than one potty stop per trip. That's what God made empty Coke bottles for.

9. HOARDER: Your husband will know if anything happens to his good old college sweatshirt covered in his good old college stains, he will never be able to exercise again. Also, the second you throw away that take-out container with the cure for cancer he's been culturing in the back of the fridge, it will trigger the immediate meltdown of polar icecaps. As you sit on your roof, waters rising around you, he'll be forced to point out it's all your fault. If only you hadn't tossed that leftover Kung Pao Chicken, you could have held out until help arrives. And if only you hadn't gotten rid of that special sweatshirt he needed for his workout routine, he would be in good enough physical shape to turn the rowing machine and one of the bathtubs into a rescue boat. If only.

8. LAUNDRY: Very bad case scenario–he might expect you to do his laundry. Even worse case scenario—he will do your laundry.

7. FEMALE SYMPATHIZER WANNABE: Take your average millennial husband. He knows PMS is out there, his enemy, waiting to turn a relatively rational wife into someone whose reply to "Hello," is "What do you mean by that, you Neanderthal?" He also knows that even to suggest, "That time of the month?" and he could be on sofa-sentry until sometime next century. If he's lucky. Will this stop him from asking, "Touch of the old hormones?" Of course it won't. (But it might help your defense when you're trying to get the homicide charges reduced to involuntary manslaughter…)

6. BODILY FLUID REJECTOR. (No, I didn't mean *those* bodily fluids. Get your mind out of the gutter, woman…) Men, for the most part, cannot clean up vomit. That's why they go far, far away for spring break and guys' weekends. Because what's upchucked in Vegas gets cleaned up in Vegas–by someone else. So be prepared, ladies: if you get married, your child will not cough, blow, wipe, or barf on anyone but you.

5. GUILT SPREADER: Your mother-in-law might be the Travel Agent of the Year on the Grandparent Guilt Trip Express. But read the fine print before you start shopping for that Blue Almonds Moses Basket. It starts with the episiotomy, and next thing you know your single-digit clothing size, ability to stand without swaying an invisible child on your hip, or to speak in full sentences is gone. Suddenly your kids get all the good lines, while you open your mouth and out comes your mother. It really puts owning a cat into perspective.

4. PHOTOGRAPHER: Husbands have strange ideas about what makes the perfect photo. He will look through a camera's viewfinder and take the shot *even if it does not contain a single child or close relative*. If forced to photograph members of your immediate family, he will spend so long waiting for all eyes to open and all fingers to be removed from bodily orifices that the children will have grown two sizes and wandered into another zip code before the shutter clicks. Thanks to the freedom of digital cameras with exceptionally large SD cards, most women know you should click the shutter nonstop on the off-chance that a child you are related to will wander past the viewfinder. A little photoshop magic and voila! Perfect shot.

3. PERSONAL HYGIENE INNOVATOR: How do men know these things? Is it possible some mother gathers her little males and tells them, "Boys, your wife will need reminders that there is a man around the house, so be sure to leave the toilet seat raised, the manly underwear on the heater, and your very personal athletic gear looped over the towel rack. Oh, and come out and talk to her while you're flossing your teeth. Wives love that."

2. LITTLE HELPER: Many husbands see marriage as a partnership. They're willing to do their fair share–as long as it's not anything that has to be done at a defined time, or where their hands get wet. Or if it involves bodily fluids of course. (*see #6 above*) For example, with encouragement he will ~~clean the kitchen, clear the table, load the dishwasher,~~ rearrange the dirty dishes on the counter. When it comes to cooking, he'll ~~willingly peel vegetables, cut up dead chickens, chop the onions, and~~ pierce the film. Luckily, he knows the Kitchen Fairy will handle the rest. You didn't know about the Kitchen Fairy? Her little sister, the Bathroom Fairy, is the one who replaces toilet paper on the spindle. She also knows the magic spell to make the vacuum turn on.

The top reason not to get married?

1. YOU'RE ALREADY PLAYING HOUSE.

- *Our grandmothers:* "Why would a man buy an entire cow when milk is so cheap?

- *Our daughters:* "Well, why would a woman buy an entire pig for 4 1/2 inches of sausage?"

**The funny thing about this list? It contains all but one of the ten top reasons FOR men to get married.*

Editorial Note from Barb: Of course, marriage is a crap-shoot where the odds are all against you. But I took that bet over thirty years ago, and I've been winning ever since. You can too. (Except for the part where he helps with your laundry. Don't go there.)

◆ ◆ ◆

Chapter 17: Top Ten Reasons For Men To Get Married

Recently, I wrote about the top ten reasons not to get married (for women). Several people have asked for equal time for men, so here goes.

Your mother told you. Your friends warned you. Study after study showed you the facts: men who are married are richer and healthier. They live longer too. (No, it doesn't just seem that way...)

This is the point where the dedicated unmarried bring up the relationship stories like, "*Southern California woman convicted of cutting off the penis of her then-husband and throwing it into a garbage disposal.*" [No, I SO did not make that one up. http://edition.cnn.com/2013/06/28/justice/california-penis-knifing/index.html]

Okay, guys, you can uncross your legs now. And actually, the odds are with you. Even though 50% of marriages end in divorce, the vast majority of those do not involve genital reattachment surgery. Moving on...

In addition to making men richer, healthier, and older, there are other advantages to marriage. Here are my ten top reasons for men to get married:

10. Sex. You'll get regular sex without paying for dinner or pretending to enjoy chick flicks.

9. Married men know the uterus is a tracking device. Y-chromosomes keep men from being able to move their eyeballs away from the item directly in front of them—unless it is wearing a bikini—or locate items covered by other items. (Guy: "Honey, do you know where we keep the milk? Or the baby?)

8. Fatherhood. Sure, you can accomplish it without marriage. But look what you miss out on:

- *Toys.* Kids have much better ones these days, and Dad gets to play with them.

- *Trains*. Dads have been known to spend decades in the basement, "working on the kids' trains".

- *You get to embarrass your kids*. And the best part is you don't have to do a damn thing. Breathing pretty much nails it.

7. Sex. Faking it. Guys can't. Wives will. There really isn't much more to say here.

6. Power tools. You'll get them. If you've got a yard bigger than your bathroom, you'll need a power mower, preferably kind you ride on, with interchangeable attachments that can double as a military vehicle in case of World War III. Married men need and deserve them.

5. Sex. Well, yeah.

4. The Kitchen Fairy and Bathroom Fairy will move in. Be especially nice to the Bathroom Fairy, because she knows the magic to make the vacuum turn on. The Kitchen Fairy is great too. Even though you're a modern millennial-type guy who knows you'll have to share the TV remote (eventually) and you're perfectly willing to ~~cook a meal~~ pierce the film, the Kitchen Fairy has magic spells passed down through the ages for producing food in pots and pans. If it makes you feel better, you should know that the Fairies really, really want you there. Who else would whap the spiders?

3. Shopping. No, you'll still have to do it. But you'll never have to make another decision again, even about her present because she'll tell you exactly what to get there too. Win-win.

2. You won't grow old and die alone and two weeks later when the neighbors complain about the smell, they'll find you, sitting with your old bathrobe gaping open, with flies on your eyeballs and your dog eating exposed parts of your anatomy. So there's that. *[Oops, sorry guys! Tell you what — just keep those legs crossed. We're almost done here...]*

And what is the top reason for men to get married (other than being richer, healthier, getting lots and lots of sex, and never having to worry about remembering your mother's birthday, because the Kitchen and Bathroom Fairies are all over that one)?

1. The future. You'll be with the one person who fell in love with you when you were younger, cooler, and had more hair. And she still sees you that way.

And there's the sex thing.

❖ ❖ ❖

Chapter 18: Men & Women. Still Needs Work.

Really long intro:

There was a video making the rounds on Facebook, a collection of clips from Hollywood movies of *"women who needed a spanking"*.

I know. I couldn't watch it either, and I'm certainly not going to link to it, even if its point is that things used to be worse.

But it did get me thinking about the ways some things have actually changed or are changing. For one thing, outside of specifically labeled BDSM mainstream films [cough, *Fifty Shades*, cough, cough], men hitting women "who need it" isn't really a positive Hollywood thing these days. Mom-shaming is out, and so (supposedly) is body-shaming. Same-sex marriage is legal, and gender pay equality is at least the law (if still pretty far from the reality).

I have a son-in-law who leaps up and has dishes done before we even set down our forks. I have a daughter who actually understands how those little cartoon guys in the directions want us to put together flat-pack furniture. I have a husband who makes the bed every morning—although, if I'm still in it, he makes it right over me. Even a p**sy-grabbing POTUS has at least led to #MeToo, toppling tinpot abusers from their entitlement thrones and providing women with strength in numbers.

But still... I have a new granddaughter, and I'd really like to believe that she'll grow up to make as much money as any grandsons I may have. I'd like to think she could take a bus home at night without having to keep her keys between her fingers as a weapon, or walk down a street without people whistling at her and telling her to smile. And most of all, I'd like her to be able to take all the jobs and trips and adventures she wants, instead of those where she would be 'safe'.

I want all the big things for her, but I'd also like to hope that things will improve in a couple of teeny little areas that still need work. All progress considered, this blast-from-the past from my 1990s newspaper column in *The Champaign-Urbana News Gazette* is not nearly as dated as it should be in the new millennium.

❖ ❖ ❖

"Men and women, women and men. It will never work."—Erica Jong

I am certain his mother never mentioned that it's unmanly to wipe off kitchen counters, but almost every guy knows it. He also knows he doesn't need to wash the pots and pans because the Fairy Godmother of the Kitchen will handle that. You remember the Fairy Godmother? She also goes into the bathroom occasionally to put a new roll of toilet paper on the spindle, although her reasons for doing so remain a mystery to him.

Did some mother sit her little males down and tell them, "When you're big boys, you'll want to spend all your waking and most of your sleeping time thinking about the two things which start with 'S', one of which is not 'sports'?

Or like me, did she sit down with her little females and tell them, "Play with these toy trucks and tools, symbols of your brave new world?" The symbols remained untouched by Daughters #1 and #2. Then my son was born, and even before he could crawl, testosterone-poisoning dragged him over to one of those trucks and evoked the primal comment, "*Rrrrrrrrrrunnnnn.*"

A few years later, my four-year-old daughter was playing superheroes with two little boys. "No sexism here," I congratulated myself.

"Hey, Wonder Woman," bellowed Superman. "Make me and Batman some dinner."

[I did take some tiny amount of comfort in the fact that Wonder Woman bellowed back, "Nuke it yourself. I'm writing."]

Once I went to see the show designed and presented by the children in my son's preschool class. First the little girls donned tutus and pirouetted to "The Sugarplum Fairy" from *The Nutcracker*. Next the little boys presented their version of *"You Ain't Nothing but a Hound Dog."* Like their model—not to mention most males between the ages of birth and death—the little Elvises devoted only about two-percent of their attention to the guitars they'd made out of rubber-bands and cardboard boxes, reserving their real concentration (and at least one hand at any given time) for monitoring the status of their Family Jewels.

Men do not, I'm sure, have any easier time figuring out women. I remember my father shaking his head and telling his eight daughters, "Girls, whatever you do, don't grow up to be women."

Back when I was in high school, our nuns would whisper to us that boys were different.

"They have needs," said Sister Mary Phys-Ed during PE/Sex Ed.

"They can't control those needs," continued Sister Mary-Library during English/Sex ed.

"You have to be strong for both of you,' said Sister Mary-cafeteria during Study Hall/Sex Ed.

"Pray for purity," Said Sister Mary-Arithmetic during Math/Sex Ed.

Our scholarly instincts demanded that we test this hypothesis. Thoroughly.

But just then we got liberated and found out we had needs too. At first, ours weren't any more interesting than theirs were. But then we discovered PMS and The Biological Clock, the two greatest weapons in the war of the hormones since the headache.

For example, consider the scene at a typical party.

Cinderella: Hello, I'm doubled over with PMS-induced tension from spending my days clawing my way through the testosterone-dominated corporate world without sacrificing my feminine power. According to my enchanted basal thermometer, you only have until my biological clock strikes midnight to make a lifelong commitment to developing sensitivity to my needs, fathering my child, and guaranteeing that I live happily ever after."

Prince: So, how about those Seahawks?

Fairy Godmother: Given where Cinderella stuck that enchanted thermometer, I think it's safe to say this story did not end happily ever after.

None of this helps get toilet paper onto the spindle, but at least it might convince the Prince that the Fairy Godmother REALLY wants it there.

◆ ◆ ◆

PART 3: LIFE

♦ ♦ ♦

Chapter 19: Top Five Reasons Why The Paleo Diet Is The End Of Civilization As We Know It:

Several celebrities have been touting the benefits of the Caveman Paleo diet. The idea is that if we eat the way people did 10,000 years ago, we will all be much healthier. As scientist Christina Warriner explained in her TED Talk, they couldn't be more wrong. But she missed a few points, so I'd like to point out the top five reasons why the Paleo Diet will lead to the end of the world.

Reason #5: <u>No variety.</u> Since Airstream trailers weren't invented yet, cavemen couldn't take their freezers on the road after they ate all the local food and annoyed all the local neighbors by drawing graffiti antelopes on the local cave walls. So their menu was limited to slow rabbits, slower fish, and berries that didn't kill them first.

Reason #4: <u>Paleo diet is dangerous.</u> Paleolithic lettuce was pretty much all thorny spines, and the carrots were woody spikes (useful only if you encounter prehistoric vampires). And the diet Coke was unsweetened.

Why Paleo Lifestyle Was So Difficult

Reason #3: <u>PMS.</u> With no chocolate (no beans, including cocoa), no milkshakes (no dairy because those mastodons were really unpleasant about the whole milking concept), and not even any salt pretzels (no gluten), the stone age was a scary place.

Reason #2: <u>They're all dead.</u> If the paleo diet was so healthy, why was the caveman life expectancy at birth only 33 years? (No, you mathematical types— you can just stop right there. You know who you are. Not only do I NOT want you to make my English-major brain contemplate the actual statistical skew caused by the ginormous infant mortality figures, but I also don't want all those cavemen-fundamentalists picketing my blog with their Cavebabies-Are-People-

Too signs...)

Reason #1: <u>And the top reason why the Caveman Paleo Diet would be the end of civilization as we know it?</u> No coffee beans means no Starbucks, so nobody would have a venue for their info-interview at a Silicon Valley startup, so there would be no internet development, so mobile phones wouldn't have broadband apps, so you couldn't look up the nearest paleo restaurant serving only gluten-free, high-protein grass-fed meat, plus organically raised nuts and non-genetically-modified berries. So basically everyone on the Paleo Diet would starve to death. In addition to no cellphones or internet, we won't have any Scotchy Scotch Scotch Ben & Jerry's, caramel-macchiatos, or cronuts. I'm pretty sure this is mentioned in several versions of the End of Days.

Plus Miley Cyrus does Paleo.

❖ ❖ ❖

Chapter 20: 15 Things I'm Not Giving Up To Be Happy

After the third friend recommended Luminita D. Saviuc's article, <u>Fifteen Things You Should Give Up to Be Happy</u>, I decided to take a look. The first thing I noticed was that 447,611 people had already 'liked' it on Facebook alone. If you don't count books with "Fifty Shades" or "Hunger Games" in their titles, that's more people than bought anything on the top seller lists in 2012. It's even more people than *like* Facebook pages of Pope Francis, Queen Elizabeth, and President Obama (not counting the ones with pictures of First-Dog Bo, or the Duchess of Cambridge's baby bump of course).

And all 447,611 of them are wrong. People give stuff up for Lent, to be miserable or something. It's called a sacrifice, for which *The Oxford Dictionaries* provides the following definition:

Sacrifice*:*

- *An act of slaughtering an animal or person or surrendering a possession as an offering to a deity*
- *An animal, person, or object offered in the act of sacrifice*
- *An act of giving up something valued for the sake of something else regarded as more important or worthy*

With the exception of a couple of people I would happily offer as sacrifices, guess what's not mentioned here? You got it: my happiness. Based on the above definition, I can only think of two reasons for me to make a sacrifice. Reason #1: the chance to win obscenely big prizes. (*Yes, Monty, I'll sacrifice the washer/dryer and year's supply of dog shampoo I've already won for what's behind door number three.*) Reason #2: someone who shares my bed or my DNA needs me. (*Yes, I'll gnaw off my own hand to help my child on the off-*

chance that s/he will serve up some grandchildren someday.)

The article goes on to list no fewer than fifteen (*15!*) things to give up. So let's just take a look at the happiness bonanza if we make those fifteen sacrifices.

Sacrifice #1. Give up your need to always be right. But it doesn't make me the least bit happy to be wrong (which is pretty much what happens when you're not right).

Sacrifice #2. Give up your need for control. It's true that my offspring often refer to me with the C-word (control-freak). Like it's a bad thing. Like my world wouldn't be a better place if everyone would just do things my way. For example, a few years ago, I was called for jury duty. It was the worst possible time to leave work, but I actually wanted to do it. My smug glow of civic virtue lasted until I met the rest of the jurors. Somehow several newly-minted teenaged voters were called for jury duty and made it onto the same panel. (Full disclosure: at first the rest of us old-farts were so charmed by their enthusiasm, we even went along with one young man's request to serve as foreman. As my grandmother would say, no good deed goes unpunished.)

The trial was straightforward and everyone knew their role. The defendant, while sentenced to home-detention at his mother's house, had removed his monitor and was recaptured months later. He admitted to leaving detention, explaining that his mother's house was in a noisy neighborhood and her TV cable service was cancelled. But he wanted to return to house arrest instead of being sent to prison, so he'd requested a jury trial. We jurors returned to our little room, relieved that we'd done our duty with this open-and-shut case and would soon be back at work.

That's when the young jury foreman and his two-angry-boy-sidekicks detoured into TV-La-La Land. "What if the defendant hadn't called his parole officer because he was afraid of The Man?" asked one.

"What if there were rival gang members at the prison who would attack him?" added another.

"What if he knew the police were corrupt—everyone knows that, right?—and so he was afraid to turn himself in?" triumphantly finished our feckless foreman.

What if *three friggin days* of this went on while the clueless baby-jurors who had nothing better to do— because college freshman orientation didn't start for several weeks, plus Mom was still cooking their dinners and doing their laundry, while TV was just summer reruns—debated these points with unflagging enthusiasm? Finally on the afternoon of Day Three, as the God-help-us-if-this-kid-represents-our-country's-future Jury Foreman launched into yet another rehash of a plot he'd seen on CSI, I snapped.

"Stop. Right. There."

Three young heads shot up in shock. Who let A Mother in there while they were playing grownup?

It was my *You're going to eat your vegetables and you're going to do it NOW* voice. "I've had just about enough. We're going to go around this table and we're each going to say one word. If you think the defendant took off his monitor and skipped–as we all heard him admit doing–then the word you are going to say is *'guilty'*. If you think he lied about doing that, then you are going to say *'not guilty'*."

The young man opened his mouth (probably to tell me that *'not guilty'* is two words) but stopped when I pointed to the hand he could tell it to. "Not one more word out of you until this is done. Nod if you understand me." His colleagues wouldn't meet his eye so he shrugged.

[Eye-roll.] "Whatever." *[More eye-roll.]*

I pulled out a list of each of our names and made two columns next to them. "Fine. I'll start. Guilty." We went around the table, each person echoing me. When it came to our fearless Foreman at the end, he started to say, "But…"

I held up the hand again. "Did he do it?"

The young man rolled his eyes.

"Say it."

[Eye-roll, sigh, eye-roll] "Guilty."

As we were leaving, the prosecutor came out to talk to us. The Defense attorney's only strategy, he said, had been to try to get as many of the young students onto the panel as possible in hopes that they would see themselves as crusaders against The Man. One of the other jurors nodded. "It might have worked, if that Mom over there hadn't sent them to time-out and made them play nice."

Chalk one up for the control-freak.

Sacrifice #3. <u>Give up on blame.</u> I never blame anybody. Unless they deserve it. Or I just plain don't like them.

Sacrifice #4. <u>Give up the past.</u> If you love something, let it go. If it comes back to you, it's probably something you gave birth to who wants to move back in with you. Or a pizza. A moment on your lips, and your hips are never going give up the past pizza…

Lots More Sacrificial... Give up on... Well actually, I just skimmed the rest of them. They got repetitive, and pretty much fell into my 'If I ain't broke, don't fix me' category. So there you have it. I'm pretty happy and I didn't have to give up a damn thing. Now alsl I have to do is sit back and wait for 447,611 people to *like* this on Facebook...

◆◆◆

Chapter 21: Barb's Secret Ninja Method To Declutter Everything. (EXCEPT Linen Closets.) You're Welcome.

"Only two skills are necessary to successfully put your house in order: the ability to keep what sparks joy and chuck the rest, and the ability to decide where to keep each thing you choose and always put it back in its place."
— Marie Kondō, Spark Joy: An Illustrated Master Class on the Art of Organizing and Tidying Up, (Ten Speed Press; 2016)

Several friends are reorganizing their lives according to Organizational Empress Marie Kondo's dictates. It's an intense discipline. As a teenager, Marie Kondo's OCD obsession with tidying up was so consuming, she actually blacked out. While unconscious, she heard a voice proclaiming the tenets of her new organizational system. (Don't judge: thanks to those voices, she's a multi-millionaire today.)

There are two reasons why this would never work for me. First, of course, is the whole hearing-voices-while-unconscious thing. Except for certain pharmaceutically-enhanced occasions which we'll skip over, my only other unconscious experience involved a middle-of-the-night attempt to paint our (pink) kitchen cabinets, only to find myself somehow on the floor with the dog licking my face. But all the voice in my head (which sounded suspiciously like my mother) communicated was a strong conviction that cabinets should be painted by someone else. [For some reason my subsequent book *"Let Someone With Better Medical And More Life Insurance Do It"* didn't make the bestseller lists. Go figure.]

But the real reason the Kondo method wouldn't work for me is of course, my mother. If anything sparked in her house, it was immediately covered with electrical tape and plugged right back in. If a possession didn't fill one of her ten children with joy, it was taken back and handed down to the next child in line. We learned early to be demonstrably joyful about anything that came our way—and then to immediately hide whatever it was.

Growing up in the days before engineers like my father found their spiritual homeland in Silicon Valley, my family travelled from town to town with other nomadic engineering families selling their slide rules to the highest bidder. In each new place, my parents would buy the closest thing to the same two-story colonial house. (Easier than it sounds, because in those days builders were covering California with exactly two housing designs: single-story ranch and two-story colonial.) Mother would deal out the paintbrushes to any offspring tall enough to wield them, and every surface would be painted—usually Navajo White—after which she'd slot all possessions into the exact same places as their previous two-story (Navajo White) colonial. Organization job done, and if anyone felt joy or sparks, they put it down to running out of fabric softener and/or my brother messing with the wiring again.

Time passed, and soon I was welcoming my parents to my own (non-colonial) house following the birth of Child#1. My mother was the kind of person who you would swear was giving her full attention to your heart-to-heart talk, only she was somehow also completely cleaning your kitchen. By the time you warmed up to your main rant, she was warming up lunch, defrosting something for dinner, and sorting out the Ha-Ha** drawer.

[Every kitchen has a Ha-Ha—the drawer that starts life with the hopeful/unlikely job of organizing take-out menus or dish towels, or randomly essential matches, candles, batteries, etc. After about a week of religiously observing this role, the drawer mysteriously fills up with...everything else, achieving packing density that would make Tetris masters weep.]

On this particular maternal visit, I was feeding the baby while my mother chatted with me, made my bed, did the laundry, folded the clothes, and headed upstairs. Too late, I realized my mistake! I couldn't move fast enough to intercept before she opened the upstairs cupboard we optimistically referred to as the linen closet.

Silence.

I strained to hear...anything.

More silence.

Some minutes later, she came into my room. "I guess you've been too busy with the baby and everything to organize your linen closet."

I nodded, trying to look pathetically busy instead of like the type of person whose linen closet looks like bombs went off in there on a regular basis.

"So I refolded everything."

Now I tried to look like the person whose linens had ever even been introduced to folding as a concept.

"And sorted it all according to sheet size, bedroom, and color."

I gave up on even trying to look like I would—in an alternate reality—sort linens according to color and function, let al*one a*ccording to joy-sparking. After all, she'd given birth to me, plus she'd already seen my Ha-Ha drawer.

When Mother left, of course, the closet resumed its impersonation of the trailer park aprés-tornado. This lasted until the day Child#4 channeled her grandmother and organized the linen closet as my Mother's Day present. Separate bins and shelves were hand-labeled according to her version of their function:

- Kids' Sheets (with stupid characters we outgrew a decade ago but Mama won't get rid of).

- Mama's White Sheets (She eats vanilla ice cream too. Just sayin'.)

- Ratty Old Towels Mama Makes the Kids Use.

- Guest Towels Too Good for the Peasants Who Actually Live Here** [**plus additional label with NOTE: DO NOT even think of touching Guest Towels because Mama says quick death would be too easy for you and she knows how to make you suffer.]

- Guest Sheets** [**yet another additional label with NOTE: See Guest Towel note. Mama says she knows where you sleep.]

I thought that kid would never leave home, but at last she headed off to collect her (engineering, of course) degree. The linen closet and I breathed a sigh of relief and vowed never to organize anything again.

"But wait," you protest. "What about what you promised in the title? Your secret ninja-method to declutter everything?"

I'm a professional writer. I didn't forget a thing. The 800 words I've written so far were just foreshadowing. Yeah, that's it.

Fact is, my friends' new life-changing obsessive compulsive religious frenzy decluttering didn't interest me until I read that Ms. Kondo's books, consulting, and each organized breath brings in millions of dollars and even more in yen every year. Holy spark of joy! So I decided to ~~look into getting my hands on some of that income~~ share my organizing secrets with you. My new book, *Declutter for Fun & Profit,* tells the gut-wrenching story of the years I spent worrying whether that feeling in the pit of my stomach was my possessions sparking joy or just those super-sized lunch tacos getting ready to blow (in which case we'd better all hope no sparking occurs).

I know none of us wants some huge book cluttering up their place, so I've written all my decluttering secrets in graphic manga format, printed on toilet paper for easy and functional er… disposal.

EXCERPT: **Barb's Manga Guide to Instant Decluttering for Fun (yours) and Profit (mine)**

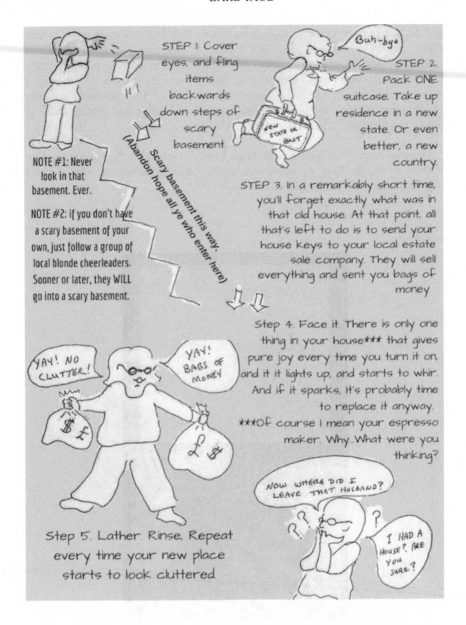

—100% GUARANTEED not to cause additional clutter because it's printed on toilet paper.

I know the Kondo method says you should touch each thing and calibrate its joy spark potential. But let's face it...you own a LOT of crap and there's dust and probably spiders. That's why your place is so cluttered. (And even if you did get sparked, you probably just need a humidifier.) Plus you're supposed to roll each spark-worthy item so that it stands up in your drawers. Seriously. Life's *way* too short for rolling bras. You'll have plenty of time to roll underwear and sort your linen closet when you're old and you've completely given up all hope of anything interesting happening in your life like Daniel Craig calling to whisk you away to a tropical island paradise for some uh-huh, uh-huh.

I'd like to give you more pointers or the contact number for a really good travel agent, but Daniel just called and I've got to head out. Uh-huh, uh-huh!

❖ ❖ ❖

Chapter 22: To My Mother & Daughters: "Sorry About... You Know... The World."

For the past year, I have done very little work on my current writing projects. We bought a house, and for the first time I felt like I understood my mother.

Mother had her first five children in six years. Someone asked her about that childless year in the middle. "That was the year," explained Mother, "we bought the house." The Year Of The House included but was not limited to:

- My brother falling into the hole being dug for the new basement bathroom (broken collarbone)

- My attempting to slide down a bannister which stopped halfway down the stairs even though I didn't (stitches in chin)

- My brother running his arm through the wringer-washer (skin grafts)

- My sister releasing the handbrake on their first new car (totaled—the car, not the sister)

I can only assume my parents were too numb after The Year Of The House to really consider the consequences of producing five additional children. By my calculations this meant:

- 7 1/2 years of pregnancy.

- 62,050 arguments about why we couldn't have Neon Chocolate Frosted Glow-in-the-Dark cereal for breakfast when the TV *promised* it was nutritious and satisfying.

- 1,750 loaves of bread, 875 jars of jam and enough peanutbutter to finance Jimmy Carter's presidential campaign got soggy in 21,000 sack lunches and were thrown into 21,000 trash cans.

- 14,235 dinners refused by children who would only eat spaghetti, hamburgers, and pizza.

- 234 Parent-Teacher Association meetings attended so nobody would elect Mother president in her absence. (This actually happened when an unexpectedly early labor put her in the hospital during the PTA election.)

- 360 parent-teacher conferences where she held her tongue even when the teacher young enough to be her daughter confided the five-year-old was "immature".

- 21,000 "Have you finished your homework yet?" questions. And even worse, 21,000 answers.

- 40 years of college tuition.

And for all this, what did Mother get?

303 Mother's Day cards, 174 bottles of bad perfume, and some of the worst breakfasts-in-bed in recorded history. Then, when she was in no condition to defend herself, we presented her with our gifts. One of our favorite presents was perfume, although it was somewhat confusing to purchase. We noticed the more you paid, the less you got. We got a *lot*.

Around middle school, I decided Mother could use a little more glamour. A sales clerk showed me a gown and robe billowed in ruffles, chiffon and lace.

"It's a pen-wore," I informed my skeptical siblings.

"A pen-*what?*"

"Not a *what*." I tried to explain because I needed their financial assistance in the project.

"Who wore it?"

"Pen-wore, *PEN-WORE!*" I knew I was losing the battle. "And don't ask me who 'Pen' was."

"P-E-I-G-N-O-I-R." Mother's voice floated down the stairs. "And I don't want one. How about some perfume?"

So Mother, I owe you an apology for that year's exceptionally large Mother's Day bottle that smelled like a morgue. And for taking so long to understand about The Year Of The House. Oh, and the Equal Rights Amendment. I'm *really* sorry about that one.

And to my daughters, nieces, and their daughters: I also owe all of you an apology. When you were babies, we said you could grow up to be anything you wanted. We lied. You can't grow up to be president of the United States. You can't expect to make the same amount as a man (unless you can wait until the year 2053). And if you shoot for those things, or even if you mention the obstacles in your way?

My own daughter, journalist Amanda Taub, addressed it in her article for Vox on Bernie Sander's sexist, misogynist supporters, the BernieBros. The conversation about whether Bernie's supporters are heroes or trolls who could affect the presidential race was, Amanda argued, a red herring.

> *"When Hillary Clinton gets criticized for "shouting," even though Bernie Sanders is beloved for speaking in a register that seems calculated to drown out every Goldman Sachs banker in a 5-mile radius, we know what that really means—and that it means the same thing for us. When we hear that she's not "likable," we know what that really means—and what it means for us. When we hear that she's bossy, we know what that really means—and what it means for us."*—Amanda Taub for Vox, http://www.vox.com/2016/2/5/10919754/bernie-bro-sexism

It's not about the gender pay gap. It's about the gender-coded messages that say it's fine for women to make it to the top, as long as they know their place and have great hair and the right shoes and don't mind warping their children's lives with their utter failure to nurture them.

So I'm sorry. I hope you don't mind that we didn't fix the world. Or that you can't, in fact, have it all, or even what the man in the next desk over can expect to have. I hope you do a better job on this than we did. I hope you do it before your daughters have to figure out why it's only women who have to ask how to have it all.

Oh, and I hope you don't give your mother perfume for Mother's Day. She'd really rather have the Equal Rights Amendment. Or a nice bottle of El Dorado rum for her mojitos. Just sayin…

To my parents and my kids— I'm SO sorry about the whole world. Except for chocolate. And coffee, of course.

❖ ❖ ❖

Chapter 23: Top Ten Great Reasons To Get Older.

Every time I go to New York, I learn something new. Last time, I learned I'm one of these people.

PRIORITY SEATING: Please offer your seat to a pregnant woman. Unless she's wearing a Red Sox hat.

I know that because every single time I got onto a subway, people leaped up to offer me their seat. My baby is a college graduate, and the only happy event I'm expecting is the release of the new iPhones. So that leaves me as the three-legger. Wait… WTF?

See, I think of myself as a relatively sophisticated city-savvy chick. But apparently, in the light from the New York subway system, I'm the chick's geriatric granny, unable to stand and probably not so good with the hearing either. But do you think for one minute I'd admit to undeserved and unnecessary impersonation of a senior citizen? Hell, yeah. That 'priority' seat was mine.

That's when it hit me. There are actually some *good* things about getting old.

I haven't made an exhaustive list yet, but here are a few I've just come up with.

Not even counting the fact that it certainly beats the alternative, the top ten great things about getting older are:

10: On vacation, your energy runs out *before* your money does.

9. Nobody expects you to learn things the hard way so you can build character.

8. You don't sweat the small stuff (and not just because you can't see it any more without your good glasses—which you haven't seen in months and so you mostly just wear the ones from the Dollar Store that you buy by the dozen).

7. Old people get released first in hostage situations. (Probably because the terrorists get tired of being told to "Speak up young man!")

6. You can mess with your kids' heads by telling them you've decided to sell your house, buy a boat, and sail around the world. (Bonus points for working the phrase "In my remaining years" into that conversation.)

5. Senior discounts. People just look at you and knock off 15%.

4. You start to feel like you're getting your money's worth out of all that medical insurance you've been paying for all these years. This is an important topic that you feel certain everyone around you would like to hear more about. Much more…

3. Stretch trousers: your middle-finger salute to the Fashion Police.

2. It's so easy to get laughs. Just use very modern slang, mention your latest social media app or Stories on Snapchat, or talk about a GIF you made—but end each sentence with "Dear" or "Sweetheart".

And the top reason it's great to get old?

1 . Even though your memory has always been crap and you've been forgetting things all your life, now people just chuckle about "senior moments" and totally forgive you.

[NOTE: On the way to the airport the next day, two young men politely argued over which one should offer me his seat. Another man asked if I was going to the airport—you think it was the suitcase?—and stood nearby so he could tell me when I was within two stops because the speakers weren't working. Geezerhood rocks!]

Chapter 24: Won't You Be My (CREEPY) Neighbor?

My daughter and I were heading home from the movie when the police stopped us at the entrance to our little slice of McBurbia. "There's been," they informed us, "...a Situation."

I tried to explain it to them—I absolutely *had* to get home or in about nine months there could be a Situation at my house. My son and his girlfriend had left the theater before us and were undoubtedly back at the house already. You could practically see the hormone clouds from the bottom of the hill where we were stopped. In fact, I could look up that hill and see the only lights on in our house were in the spa room. You know, the one with the hot tub I tried to get the last owners to take with them because we were from the Midwest. (We do hot dish, not hot tub.)

I tried to tell the nice officer I wasn't ready to be a grandmother. Almost two hours went by. The spa room dimmed, as if the only lights left on were those under the water surface in the hot tub. I started picking out baby names. When we finally made it back to the house, two innocent (but slightly damp) teenagers insisted that they had just been sitting around wondering what kept us. And hey, how weird was it that neither of their mobiles had registered incoming calls or texts. LOTS of texts.

Next day I discovered the delay Situation was because our next-door neighbor had met some process-servers at her door with a display of the weapons her gun-dealing current gentleman caller kept around. I should explain that our neighborhood was like some Walt Disney version of ultimate suburbia, so this neighbor was a bit... different. The day we moved in, she came over to make sure we weren't anything undesirable like Asians or Jews. (I told her she'd hit paydirt–we were both, and were thinking of renting out the basement to a black and hispanic same-sex couple.) In my defense, I didn't know she kept an arsenal in her house. A week later, we met again when we arrived home to discover that she was just cutting down the last of our row of beautiful old trees on one side of our yard. So she could keep an eye on us.

A few weeks went by after she ran off the process servers. I was over in the next town picking up my daughter when my husband called and casually suggested we might want to stop and grab a latte somewhere. Could this be the same husband who would wait in Burger King's interminable line for a crap cup of coffee rather than pander to my addiction to overpriced caffeinated beverages with fake Italian names? "Who is this really?" I asked, figuring that pod people had finally mastered the phone system.

Just then my phone buzzed a call from my son. He said people with automatic weapons and SWAT signs on their backs were pouring through the pathetic new bushes I'd just planted to replace the trees. They were heading toward our neighbor's house. He wanted me to tell his father, who was standing in the picture window, drinking a cup of awful coffee and watching the show, that maybe he should get down.

Sadly, they took my poor neighbor away and some accountants moved in instead. There went the neighborhood.

◆ ◆ ◆

Chapter 25: Reunion? Somebody Made A (BIG!) Calculation Error…

"REUNION YEAR" warns the (appropriately black) banner in the alumni newsletter, along with a number that just can't be real. Didn't we just do that? I'm pretty sure I wrote about it. Well… yes and no. I did write, but it was a newspaper column back in 1991. I'll let you do the math about which reunion is coming up this time, but meanwhile here's the blast-from-the-past, or at least from the Champaign-Urbana News Gazette in April, 1991.

◆ ◆ ◆

I'm not old enough to attend a 15th reunion.

When my first daughter was old enough to ask my age, I said I was 21. Now that she knows a bit more math, she wants to know why my parents let me go to college at eight and get married at twelve. I told her it was because I grew up in California. Here in Illinois, girls can't get married until they are 32 and have completed their PhD.

"Profession?" asked the enclosed alumni information form. I don't mind answering easy questions — name, sexual preferences, bank balance, how I got that scar way down there, etc. — but this was a tough one. When I started practicing motherhood, I didn't exactly respond to a help-wanted ad in the classifieds:

> ***Expanding organization seeks Director****. Qualifications: must know how to put toilet paper on spindle, prepare creative and interesting dishes for staff to refuse if they don't involve the words 'peanut butter' and serve as walking Kleenex to small staff members. On-call 24/7, no*

pay, no sick leave, no chance of promotion. Job security, annual recognition breakfast, company car.

For help I looked at the Reunion Directory which listed my fellow graduates and their professions. The majority were professors, doctors, attorneys, or vice-presidents. The closest to my life was the one who listed 'doorman', but my guess is he didn't mean holding closed the doors of public restroom stalls while inquiring if the occupant needs to be wiped.

Another classmate claims the title 'psychotherapist', but she probably would not agree with my behavior modification technique of sending patients to their rooms, sometimes without dessert, until they are ready to be nice. And she would probably lose her license if she tried kissing the ouchie to make it better.

Other job titles I considered:

- *Statistical Analyst.* "I don't care if 98.9% of the third-graders on the face of the planet have a later bedtime — GET IN THE BED."

- *Media consultant.* "No, you can't watch Geraldo talking to men who used to be women who used to be hookers."

- *Investment Counselor.* "I know it's your allowance, but 4-year-olds can't buy flamethrowers."

- *Fiscal Manager.* "Sure we can afford to go to Disneyland — we'll just give up luxuries like food, clothing, and the mortgage."

I considered various job titles suggested by my friends. *Housewife*, they told me, was déclassé. *Homemaker* was out because if I'd been around when my home was made, my bumper sticker could read "Life begins at 120". *Domestic Goddess* sounded promising (porcelain throne first door on your left; flush when you're done, and put the lid down please) but the only way the goddess could be the object of worshipful glances is to sit on the TV.

Another suggestion, *Domestic Engineer*, implies a degree of household competence nobody in their right mind thinks I'll ever achieve. In fact, each time I had a baby, I abandoned some aspect of domestic maintenance. First it was ironing, then cooking, and finally housecleaning. Since all that's left is personal hygiene, I think we can all hope the stork avoids Chateau Taub.

[UPDATE FROM BARB: luckily for Child#4, the stork didn't get that memo.]

I almost settled on *"Perfect"*, a job title which my mother claimed for years. I still remember how surprised Sister Mary First Grade was when I told her my father was an engineer and my mother was Perfect. The problem is that someone at my school might remember me, or even worse, have a few of my old transcripts lying around.

So at the class reception in June, when one of the doctors/lawyers/vice-presidents/doormen asks me what I do, I'll probably have to tell the truth.

"I'm a Dictator for Life. It's a tough job, but somebody's got to do it."

◆ ◆ ◆

Chapter 26: Do You Know A Hero?

"Heroes may not be braver than anyone else. They're just braver 5 minutes longer."—Ronald Reagan

When I was little, I found out about heroes. They are the ones who fight the biggest dragons, win the prettiest princesses, and save the best kingdoms in the end. This didn't surprise me in the least, because I knew someone who was a hero–my father. My mother told me.

As I got older, this belief was shaken a bit. It didn't seem like it was a hero's work to fix toilets, keep old cars running, and take your (ten!) kids out for ice cream after dinner so your wife could rest. But I was wrong. That is exactly what heroes do. Then they go to work every day, put each of those ten children through college, and make sure they get a good start in life.

But heroes also answer the call when there are other kingdoms to save. There are not many left of the ones who answered during the Second World War, but my father was one of those too. Don't get me wrong. He didn't like war or approve of something that took him away from the college education he craved. For years he never discussed it. Finally, he wrote a couple of letters and we learned a little about his war as Tech Sergeant Robert Figel, Radio Operator Gunner on the B-17 FlyingFortress *Nobody's Baby*. That was until *Nobody's Baby* lost first one engine and then another during a mission over Germany. Their goal was to make it to Switzerland because rumor had it that if you were there for the duration, you were paid well and lived like kings.

When they lost the third engine, it was clear *Nobody's Baby's* crew wouldn't be spending the rest of the war on vacation in Switzerland. So Plan B was to at least make it out of German territory. With one remaining engine, the crew frantically threw everything they could unbolt off the plane to lighten the load.

"We had to drop the ball turret and everything we could drop because we were essentially down to one engine by the time we were going in for a landing."

But they made it behind Russian lines. The entire ten-man crew, all under age 22, walked away from *Nobody's Baby*–and into locals who stripped them of their fur-lined flight gear and gave them local clothing.

Finally they made it back to Italy, but replacement uniforms weren't available.

"This one officer came by–I presume he must have been regular Army because he was so rigid–West Point kind of thing. He was so furious with me being out of uniform, and he wanted to know where I was based. So I told him Naples. Then I told him he better hurry because our base was moving to Marrakesh, Casablanca, and then Dakar. And then moving again...

He asked, 'Are you in the American Army?'

I said, 'Well, yeah.'

You know, I was willing to be compatible for a war, but about that time I felt it was a Boy Scouts sort of thing, and I didn't get all that enthused."

We asked him if he missed anything about the war and he answered seriously.

"This is the frightening thing about war. I have heard it described as a narcotic, a drug that catches up with everyone and under the fervor of patriotism gets them all enthused. That's fine when a job has to be done, but war is to be avoided as much as possible.

"In all the time in the War there was never a thought of it ending. We didn't have access to newspapers or radios so we really did not know what was going on. The end was so casual. One of the guys was walking along and said that Germany surrendered... Looking at it now, I wonder why I was not more enthused about it. The crusade syndrome: through the ages all young people want wars. Yet there was not much of that. People were not negative about the war, but it was accepted as something that had to be done.

"Really, it was a time when the country experienced its finest hour, with

exceptional cooperation from the whole country. Wherever I went people were doing their best to mentally and physically support the war effort. I think of this sometimes when I see so many that do not vote. What a contrast to citizenship during the War and now."

My father's health was failing. His memory wasn't what it used to be. But he's still my hero. I thank him, every member of our armed services, and all their families for their service. You are all my heroes.

Tech Sergeant Robert Figel, Radio Operator Gunner on the B-17 Flying Fortress Nobody's Baby

❖ ❖ ❖

Chapter 27: Crash Course: How To Be Sick In Bed

"The art of medicine consists in amusing the patient while Nature affects the cure."–Voltaire

I have nothing to write about because this is day nine in which I have done ab.so.lute.ly nothing. Unless you count the moaning, of course. When sick, I am a world-class moaner. Back when my children were little, it was understood: mothers don't get sick. They may have triple-digit temperatures, cough like the death scene in *La Bohème*, and pop ibuprofen like M&Ms, but as our neighbors in Virginia said, mamas don't take to the bed. They make chicken soup and do laundry.

But now the kids are grown, I'm working at home, and here's the thing: I don't know how to be sick. I tried googling *"How to be sick in bed"*. Turns out I was supposed to be doing a lot of things the past nine days. Wiki-How's list includes art projects, crafts, sewing, playing computer games, pedicures, catching up on my texting, watching all the TV programs I don't usually bother with, making to-do lists, yada yada. I didn't tick off a single box on that list. My toenails look terrible. As a fairly competitive person, it's painful to admit I'm an abject failure when it comes to being sick in bed.

So instead, I checked in with the one expert who outranks Google. I called my mother. Both she and my sister listened unsympathetically as I poured out my despair over being unable to get Nyquil™ or any simulacrum thereof here in England. I could almost feel them reaching through the Skype window to slap me upside the head. "Have you had a hot toddy?"

[Warning: here comes fever-induced digression.] I guess I'm lucky

there are 5500 miles between us, or I would have been dodging spoons. During dinners as we were growing up, my mother enforced discipline among her ten offspring through judicious spoon flinging. As my sister pointed out, Mother must have loved us, because she never threw a knife. And we knew she could throw one, because it was a skill she'd picked up as a girl on the south side of Chicago. Occasionally she used to show off her technique out in our backyard. These demos left us impressed, jealous, and a bit worried.

As soon as we hung up, I grabbed the whiskey, lemon, and honey. The smell alone brought back so many memories. Oh, yeah! *That's* how to be sick in bed. I slept like a log that night. Despite complaints from the other occupant of the marital bed about snoring that frightened the dog and set off seismographs in neighboring counties, by the next morning, I could tell I was finally getting better.

Turns out, Mother really does know best.

MOTHER'S HOT TODDY RECIPE

- 2 Tablespoons whiskey. (If you live in Scotland, you can leave off the "e" in whisky. Either way, you should probably put some into the cup too…)

- Juice of one lemon**

- Honey (generous dollop)

- Boiling water to fill cup

**There are people who put in orange slices studded with whole cloves and stir with a cinnamon stick. There are also people who order mixed drinks with little umbrellas. You know who you are.*

Rx: Take one. WTH: take several. Mother says so.

Chapter 28: Occupy Washington (TOILETS)

[I just discovered a scary thing about this column I wrote for the Champaign Urbana News Gazette back in June 1991. If you change out some words—very few words, actually—this still works. That's pretty terrifying.]

❖ ❖ ❖

I just heard the government's partial shutdown is close to resolution. Instead of cheering, I'd like to propose a different strategy for next year. Here's how it would work:

SCENE: Morning of ~~June 30, 1992~~ September 28, 2019. The Legislature wakes up and says to itself, "What a great day to enact some meaningful legislation like naming the Official State Grub (NOTE #1: this is the only bit I can't update because we already have Congress, so we don't need another National Grub...) or annexing ~~Missouri~~ Canada." Then it glances at the clock and sees it's Budget Time.

The Legislature, of course, misses the pre-game showdowns, but arrives in time to see the ~~governor~~ Senate and the Speaker of the House face-off in the finals of the Budget Bowl. The mighty contenders are fresh, the day is young, field conditions (the backs of taxpayers) are perfect.

The contest continues through the day. As the midnight buzzer sounds, ~~the governor~~ Congress proposes a draw. "Give me victory," responds ~~the Speaker~~ POTUS, "Or give me victory. People who don't get paychecks can take a lot of comfort in the fact that I'm fighting for what I believe in: power."

Sounds familiar so far? Well, I'm proposing a new ending. Everyone in ~~Illinois~~ America should meet at my house at 8:00AM on ~~June 30, 1992~~ January 20, 2019, and we'll carpool over to ~~Springfield~~ Washington.

Once we get there, we'll take up positions–lining up in front of every bathroom in the Capitol. At the front of each line will be our shock-troops, 12-year-olds with ~~iPods~~ iPads and spare powerpacks, capable of remaining in each and every Congressional bathroom for days at a time. Our battle cry, "No Budget? No Bathroom!" will resonate against every Legislative bladder.

NOTE #2: My husband favors a more historical precedent. His great-great-grandfather, Col. Shadrach Bond, was the first governor of Illinois. When he had a political disagreement with his opponent, John Rice Jones, in 1808, Bond challenged Rice to a duel with pistols. (Actual historical fact.)

In ~~1992~~ 2019, if the ~~governor~~ President and ~~the Speaker~~ Congress know that a failure to compromise will mean they have to shoot at each other at 40 paces on live C-SPAN, and that they can't even go to the bathroom first, that budget will be balanced in no time–especially since after the Bond-Rice duel, the Legislature passed an 1810 law that in case of a fatal result of a duel, all involved parties and seconds will be held guilty of murder.

I suggest everybody who reads this post should send it to all their elected representatives as fair warning that failure to pass a timely budget next year could result in their being shot, convicted of murder, and really, really, really needing to pee. The choice is theirs.

◆ ◆ ◆

Chapter 29: Voting—Civic Pride Or The Flu?

Dear Readers, We all know the time has come for us as a nation to be serious, to sit down together, and to discuss critical issues facing our country. So this week, I was going to write about my simple, foolproof yet stunningly brilliant solution to the budget deficit. But I got up early to vote this morning instead.

When the warm glow which I mistook for civic pride turned out to be the flu, I just asked myself, "Would our Founding Fathers and Mothers have let a little thing like possible pneumonia stop them from going out in subfreezing weather to vote for local school board members?"

"Actually," myself answered, "Our Founding Mothers couldn't vote, so they would have told the Founding Fathers to wake them up when the Equal Rights Amendment passed, and then gone back to sleep." (Myself tends to get snarky when I'm coming down with the flu.)

Although it took the combined efforts of a roomful of Election Judges to get my votes cast, they seemed pleased to have a customer who wasn't even a blood relative of one of the candidates. In appreciation for their efforts, I tried not to breathe any of my germs in their directions. So I was a little lightheaded when I got back to my van and noticed a stream of antifreeze under it.

As a modern, 90's kind of woman, I'm not usually intimidated by mechanical difficulties. Calling on automotive expertise culled from decades of car commercials, 90's-Woman is supposed to diagnose, "I'm driving the car that climbed Everest in blizzard on one gallon of gas. So that leak must have come from somebody parked here before me."

Maybe it was the lack of oxygen after the Everest trip, or the fever which made me violate my most sacred tenet of automotive maintenance (*"If it goes, don't ask questions"*). I raised the hood. Luckily, farsighted Japanese engineers had anticipated this danger and placed the engine in a location which factory-trained mechanics have sworn never to reveal.

Of course, because of a provision in the Selective Service Act which requires all males over the age of eighteen to raise the hood and fiddle with wires in the event of automotive distress, the engineers couldn't leave the space under the hood empty. So they filled it with a few wires and some jugs of automotive fluids.

We all carry our parents around in our heads. Frequently, for example, I open my mouth to reply to my children and out comes my mother saying, "Would you jump off a bridge just because everybody else does it?" When it comes to cars, I can hear the father in my head praying, "Please, God, make Barb keep an eye on the fluid levels."

Against my better judgement, I surrendered to my in-head father. Opening the hood, I checked the fluid levels and discovered that I was indeed the owner of the antifreeze puddle under the car. This means, dear Readers, instead of solving the budget crisis (remember the budget crisis?), I had to fit the car repairs into a day which already included:

- Refusing three kids' requests for pre-breakfast Halloween candy. "Not until you've eaten all your frozen, nutritionally bankrupt breakfast pastries," I reply firmly.

- Refusing to let my son watch Geraldo interviewing born-agin ax-murderers who have had sex-change operations.

- Driving son to preschool.

- Driving daughter with sore throat to doctor.

- Picking up son at preschool.

- Refusing to let sick daughter watch the show her brother told her about where Donahue interviews women married to born-again ax-murderers who have had sex-change operations.

- Allowing a white-coated sadist brandishing pointed instruments to scrape away sensitive tissue in the name of dental hygiene.

- Preparing the gourmet family dinner, Mystery Casserole, which has been in my freezer so long it's mentioned in my will.

- Preforming the 187 sensitive, nurturing bedtime rituals involved in inserting four kids into their respective beds.

- Repeating the rituals at increasing decibel levels until I'm screaming the sensitive, nurturing phrase, "If you get out of that bed one more time, you'll be in time-out until puberty."

Well, so much for budget deficits. Next week: my solution for universal world peace. You're welcome.

❖ ❖ ❖

Chapter 30: Male Bonding

Last week I was at home recovering from the flu I didn't have (because as everyone knows, mamas don't get sick). So when my friend called and told me to turn on the television and learn about the Men's Movement, I had to sneak up to the attic. That's were I'd moved the TV so I could instill a lifelong sense of positive values in my children through quality family interactions and board games.

[NOTE: Sadly, this has not been an unqualified success. In fact, the only future uses I can see for the values they've exhibited so far are guerrilla warfare and academic politics.]

Educators stress the importance of monitoring our children's television viewing, but this is ~~unlikely~~ ~~impossible~~ challenging because my children represent the union of two family genetic traits:

1) **Self-control.** I have none, at least when it comes to the television. Since the dawn of time, or at least the coffee-break of time, my family has been cursed with a deep, primeval need to stare at flickering lights.

> <u>Fellow Neanderthals:</u> "How come we have to spend our time hunting, gathering, evolving opposable thumbs, and learning to walk without using our knuckles while all you prehistoric Barbs sit around staring at your fires?"

> <u>Clan of the Cave Barbs:</u> "As Darwin would say (except he's not going to be born for another million years), it's survival of the fittest. Evolution is obviously pointing in the direction of short, pear-shaped *homo barbiens* adapted to sitting for extended periods of time on their

most prominent physical feature. So when that giant meteor hits the earth causing the Ice Age and obliterating the gene pool of all of you Neanderthals who've been wasting time inventing tools, art, and music, the cave-potato Barbs will be safely inside, waiting for someone to invent television so they can binge-watch boxsets of *The Walking Dead*."

2) **Channel-control.** Due to a birth defect (he was born with a Y-chromosome), the Hub is unable to watch any channel for more than three seconds. Watching with him usually sounds something like this:

"Jack, Chrissy's stuck in the bathtub again! *[click]* This may be the wrestling match of the century *[click]* Are you feeling lucky today, punk? *[click]* ...may be the football match of the century *[click]* he's dead, Jim. *[click]* Well, Sarge, this dame says...*[click]* ...my men wear Eau d'Armpit or they wear nothing at all. *[click]* God told me he wants you to send me your life savings and I'll send you this card personally touched by my *[click]* long distance pogo-stick endurance match of the century *[click]* Why, Mr. Grant! *[click]* Jim, this man is dead *[click]* Look! Up in the Sky! It's a bird! It's a plane! It's *[click]* Alistair Cooke saying, *[click]* I love what you do for me *[click]* with thunder, gale-force winds and *[click]* beds made up with plenty of manure *[click]* for the Argentine Pocket Knife throwing match of the century. The winers of this bout will go on to be *[click]* dead, Jim. Beam me up, Scotty. *[click]*"

With this as their DNA, my kids are incapable of tearing themselves away from a dogfood commercial or even pledge week on PBS.

So anyway, there I was, huddled in the attic watching males bond. These men were very upset. Some had even burned their ties. They said they were fed up with being viewed as Work Objects and not being allowed to cry when Old Yeller dies.

I checked with my editorial research department. He tells me that in the old days, guys were only supposed to want the three G's: girls, gold, and glory. Success in any of these areas was reflected by the size of your engine. (The one in your car, not the one you lie about.) On a social level, men communicated through burps and profanity. At work, they cut down on the burps.

What does today's male want? I may have missed some of the details due to the fever, but I think according to the men interviewed on this show, he wants the right to be as sensitive as Alan Alda but still drink beer. He wants to live as long as women. He wants the immediate execution of any father who abandons his son with some lame excuse about earning a living. And most confusing of all, he wants women to stop talking so much** on long-distance car trips. Several men were quite specific about this.

**[Examples of too much road conversation: "I think we left a few kids at that last rest stop." "We haven't seen a recognizable road sign since yesterday." "Could you slow down enough for me to make out some of the larger landscape features?"]

**[Examples of good conversation: "Honey, how about another sandwich?"]

Luckily the guests on the show found a way to resolve these issues. Drums. They began to beat drums which were supposed to simulate the primal heartbeat. Unfortunately, with the typical middle-class yuppie's approach to rhythm, it was more like primal cardiac arrhythmia. As they drummed, they chanted, "HOME BASE! HOME BASE!"

Really. I couldn't make this up.

Maybe the Women's Movement should adopt some of these techniques. We could give each woman a drum and a chant emphasizing her strength and her femininity. With all of us drumming and chanting, "HALF-PRICE AT SAKS! HALF-PRICE AT SAKS!" on long-distance car trips, I'll bet the ERA would be passed in no time.

Meanwhile, I'm going back up to the attic. It's almost time for Geraldo to interview a man who's had four sex-change operations and a woman who had a pork-chop surgically removed from her posterior. Now that's what I call educational television.

◆ ◆ ◆

Chapter 31: The Day I Needed A Cell Phone (YES, I'm Really That Old)

peace, *n. 1. calm and quiet, as in kids go back to school. 2. state of accord, as in kids go back to school AND baby takes nap. 3 freedom from troubling emotions or thoughts, as in kids go back to school AND baby takes nap AND you've recorded a new answering machine message: "You have reached the home of the Taubs. The 12-year-old is not able to take your call at this time, so please leave a message at the beep and she will get back to you the second she comes in the door. If you want to speak to any other member of the family, please leave a message at the beep and we will get back to you as soon as she leaves for college. —*
Barb Webster's New Parent's Dictionary, 1995

I had to be dragged, kicking and screaming, into the twentieth century. Although I now have an answering machine with a portable phone, I miss the good old days when I could complain about everybody else's stupid messages and dehumanizing machines: "Hello, you have reached the home of the Kreblitz's. In the background, you can hear our pit bull, Jugular, dismembering an intruder. Please keep that in mind if you are only calling to see if we're away from home before breaking in. Otherwise, leave a message at the sound of the beep, and have a nice day."

But I went back to using the wall-tethered phone when I realized the kids could pick up my portable phone conversations on their walkie-talkie toys:

Kids: Mom, did Shirley's husband use to be blind?

Me: No, I don't think so.

Kids: Then how come she wants a divorce just cause he sees women now?

There are other advantages to wall-phones too. For example, I can't lose either the phone or the 12-year-old because they're both attached to the end of the phone cord. (It was probably bad planning to get a cord that stretches as far as the refrigerator though.)

But despite owning a tethered phone, and despite years of complaining about people talking on their car phones, I have a confession to make. A few weeks ago, I went to visit an old friend from college days. When we got to her house, she called her nanny at the park on the cellular phone and told her to bring the kids home. We're talking jealousy. Envy. The green-eyed monster reared its ugly head and it was talking on a cellular phone.

So why do I need a cellular phone? I've been trying to come up with a good enough reason:

- I need to send it with my husband when he goes to the grocery store so he can check with me before he buys the pickled herring in anchovy sauce instead of the mayo, or substitutes the goats-milk ice cream for the Rocky Road.

- I need to take it with me when I go to yard sales, so I can check with my husband before I buy that beautiful antique desk that *almost* fits through our door or the china cabinet the size of Vermont (solid wood!) that he won't mind helping me move since he's already fathered enough children...

- Most of all, I need it so I can ~~torture~~ check on my children:

  RING-RING. "Hi, honey, it's Mom. You're out kind of late on this date. You're where? How did you run out of gas way out there? Well, don't worry—your Dad will be right out. And dear? Stay on the line."

  RING-RING. Hi, honey, it's Mom. How do you like college? What's that? Turn down your stereo; I can't hear you. Oh, you're not in your dorm? Well, why is the music so loud in the library, and why does it stay open so late? You're in whose apartment? Don't worry—your Dad will be right out on the next plane. And dear? Stay on the line."

  RING-RING. "Hi, honey, it's Mom. How's the honeymoon going? Hello? Hello, are you there? If you can hear me, don't worry—your Dad will be right out. I'll just stay on the line..."

◆ ◆ ◆

Chapter 32: Progress, Nineties-Style

"My father worked for the same firm for twelve years. They fired him. They replaced him with a tiny gadget this big. It does everything that my father does, only it does it much better. The depressing thing is my mother ran out and bought one." —Woody Allen, *"The Nightclub Years, 1964-1968"*, recorded 1972

[NOTE FROM BARB: For those who don't remember the nineties, the song of our people was the sound of a dial-up modem connecting. My theory was that a 12-year-old boy whose voice was just starting to crack and a six-pack-a-day octogenarian smoker were standing at the phone exchange and whenever someone turned on their dial-up modem, the boy would crack out a series of random beeps from the Warner Brothers Cartoon intro, the smoker would hiss and wheeze, with boy adding intermittent beeps, and then they would flip a coin to see if they should plug in the cord to the connection or drop it. I'm pretty sure that's how it worked anyway...]

My kids are embarrassed for me. They've done their best to bring me up right, only to find that I agree with Ogden Nash when he said, "Progress might have been all right once, but it has gone on far too long."

My eight-year-old, for example, is really worried about my computer, which he thinks was probably cloned from computer chips trapped in amber during the Jurassic period. While he had no sympathy for my feeble excuse that I didn't unplug my computer during a thunderstorm because I was in the hospital, in labor at the time, my son did offer to accompany me on the expedition to replace my storm-fried modem.

Arriving at Computers-R-Us, we were greeted by a young man who asked, "What kind of system do you have?" When I told him, he was impressed. "I've heard my grandfather used to have one of those in the old days, but I've never seen one myself."

When I explained about the fried modem, he asked, "How about a Fax with background send/receive at 14,400 bps group III and V.42bis/mnp protocols which achieve throughput of 57,600 bps with a 999 box voice mail system?"

"How about a salesperson who speaks human," I replied (although my son was already nodding).

My daughters, on the other hand, are more concerned about my wardrobe deficiencies. I've tried to tell them I'm sporting the new, energy-conscious environmental-friendly look. [Translation: I gave up ironing two pregnancies ago, and I only wear things with dirt on them. For evening wear, this ensemble is often accessorized with a splash of eau d'baby puke.]

I'm not sure where they developed their fashion sense. It seems only yesterday when the best you could say for their choice of outfits was they they were politically correct—equal representation for all colors, patterns, and seasons at once. The only things missing were the empty whiskey bottles and the lampshade.

I admit that I'm not a very good shopper, especially when it comes to my own clothing. When I was their age, I used to dread the moment when my mother would drag me to Chez Mall Énorme. "But I have clothes," I'd wail, pointing to my jeans with the hand-embroidered patches and my crocheted vest.

"You're not wearing patched jeans with holes in the knees to school," my mother replied as she trapped me in a dressing room by walking out with my jeans while the saleslady with the cat glasses plied me with armfuls of tasteful polyester doubleknits.

But the shopping gene must skip generations, because my two older daughters love to shop. Actually, this has its advantages. We won't need to save for college for the oldest one, because she informed me that her career goal is a job at her favorite mall store. She already has all the qualifications: she wears a single-digit size and she can transform a basic $49.95 outfit into a $49.95 outfit with $150 of accessories faster than you can say "Visa or Mastercard". For a store discount, she'd even be perky.

Last week, in honor of their favorite holiday, Back-to-School, we went clothes shopping. "Can I have these jeans?" Child#1 asked, pointing to a pair of jeans with patches and factory-installed holes in the knees.

I opened my mouth, and out came my mother. "You're not wearing patched jeans with holes in the knees to school."

"Besides," I added, "Kids today have it too easy. In my day, we didn't have some worker in a third-world sweatshop to beat up our jeans; we had to wear them out ourselves."

Just then Child#2 came out wearing a crocheted vest and a tie-dyed gauze skirt. All she needed was the lava lamp and the "Woodstock or Bust" sign.

I turned to the saleslady with the retro cat glasses. "How do you feel about polyester doubleknits?"

◆ ◆ ◆

PART 4: HOLIDAYS

◆ ◆ ◆

Chapter 33: How To Terrorize Small Children

I committed an Easter crime once. I was persuaded to dress up in a bunny costume for my daughter's preschool class. The teacher opened the door and in I teetered, six-plus feet (counting the ears) of Easter excitement. For about a nanosecond, there was complete silence while I held up my basket of plastic eggs. Then eighteen mouths were screaming for eighteen mothers, thirty-six eyes were filling with tears, and seventy-two tiny arms and legs were churning toward the door. We're not even going to discuss what happened in eighteen little pairs of undies as I single-handedly drove the roomful of preschoolers ballistic with terror.

Maybe if that whole child-soldier/ kidnapping/ warlord gig doesn't work out for him, Joseph Kony could find fulfillment dressing up as a giant bunny and appearing before unsuspecting preschoolers.

❖ ❖ ❖

Looking back, I realize that if I'd gone into work one day to find an eleven-foot tall rabbit heading for me–with no prior memo announcing, *"At 10:15AM today, staff will be terrorized by long-eared rodents twice your size,"*–I would probably not have been nearly as nice about it as those preschoolers. After all, not one of them pressed charges or pulled a weapon even though it was hunting season. In SW Virginia. I'm just lucky I didn't end up on the hood of someone's car, tied down next to Bambi.

It's not as if I didn't know better. My kids have an unbroken string of bad experiences with costume-clad adults. The first time we did the Mouse, Donald Duck waddled up to us. He was reaching out to Child#2 when she hauled off and planted him a solid one straight to his–duckness. As I hustled the kids out of there, I noticed Daisy Duck was trying to help him up despite quacking up herself. [*I'd apologize, but come on – you knew that was coming...*]

Then there was the time we were in the grocery store. My four-year-old was busy analyzing the relative merits of the candy lining the checkout lane when he was accosted by a cookie-promoting elf whose head alone was at least as tall as my son. (The concept of selling cookies using a supersized elf head is yet another reflection of the extent of the drug problem on Madison Avenue.) The elf, who seemed directionally challenged, was being guided by a handler. "How would you like to meet the elf?" the handler asked my son.

"NO!" he screamed, racing for the exit and knocking down everything in his path. "NO, no, no, no..."

"How would you like to pay for the years of therapy we're both going to need?" I asked the elf as I gave chase.

The fact is there is no real upside to costumed adults confronting my children. Take the time I brought Child#1 to see Santa in his mall chalet surrounded by several camera-waving teenaged helper elves. My daughter didn't want anything to do with the whole setup, so she tried to escape as the elves herded her toward Santa. As he leaned down to her, she grabbed the pompoms on the end of his hat and started to pull back. One of Santa's Helpers screamed, "She's pulling Santa's little balls off!" We never did get a photo of the event, because Santa had to go feed his reindeer.

◆ ◆ ◆

Chapter 34: The Twelve Days Of Christmas, Deconstructed

This was a piece I wrote for the *Wall St. Journal*. They added the illustrations and ran it 1/6/1994. Since then it's appeared on hundreds of websites, and has been attributed to several people including my (surprised) husband.

The 12 Days, Deconstructed

On the 12th day of the Eurocentrically imposed midwinter festival, my acquaintance-rape survivor gave to me,

TWELVE males reclaiming their inner warrior through ritual drumming,

ELEVEN pipers piping (plus the 18-member pit orchestra made up of members in good standing of the Musicians Equity Union as called for in their union contract even though they will not be asked to play a note...),

TEN melanin-deprived testosterone-poisoned scions of the patriarchal ruling class system leaping,

NINE persons engaged in rhythmic self-expression,

EIGHT economically disadvantaged female persons stealing milk-products from enslaved bovine-Americans,

SEVEN endangered swans swimming on federally protected wetlands,

SIX enslaved fowl-Americans producing stolen nonhuman animal products,

FIVE golden symbols of culturally sanctioned enforced domestic incarceration,

[Note: after members of the Animal Liberation Front threatened to throw red paint at my computer, the calling birds, French hens and partridge have been reintroduced to their native habitat. To avoid further animal-American enslavement, the remaining gift package has been revised.]

FOUR hours of recorded whale songs,

THREE deconstructionist poets,

TWO Sierra Club calendars printed on recycled processed tree carcasses, and a Spotted Owl activist chained to an old-growth pear tree.

◆ ◆ ◆

Chapter 35: If It's January, I Must Owe You An Apology…

One thing that amazes me about writing a weekly column is how easy it is to offend large segments of the population. For example, I wrote a column that mentioned Florida's official junior hunting season, an outgrowth of the NRA school of sociology which teaches that allowing armed children to bag their first Bambi fosters family unity and decreases the drug problem. (I could not possibly make this up.)

At the time, we were living in southwest Virginia, which is closed for deer hunting season. Offending an armed segment of that population was not one of my better ideas. Despite my proclamation that people who display the bumper sticker "*My wife says if I go deer-hunting one more time she'll leave me. Too bad, I'll miss her*" are clearly great humanitarians with a terrific sense of humor, we decided to move to another state.

I also once offended the State of New Jersey by mentioning it in print.

Then there was the column about my problems with my ancient Volvo. Yeah, I ran that in a town with exactly one Volvo repair shop, which made as much sense as telling surgeon jokes just before the anesthetic.

> *[Um… editorial correction from the Hub: The Volvo mechanics who fix Barb's car constantly are competent, friendly professionals who carry really big wrenches. It certainly is not their fault that Barb chooses to drive a vehicle which breaks down almost as often as politicians break election year promises.]*

After my column about the severe shortage of brain cells among our pets, I was served with papers in a civil suit filed by my dog charging me with "breach of ownership and defamation of dog." Frankly, I'm suspicious: I think outside agitators like that Russian wolfhound up the street put her up to it. But I expect to reach an out-of-court settlement. She agrees to drop the lawsuit in return for being allowed to live following a certain episode last spring in which she got Child#3 to open the fridge and give her the better part of a dozen eggs. Most of these she ate, and then regurgitated as usual under my dining room chair. But several she hid in thoughtful places like behind the stove and other sites which became horrifically apparent as the summer (hottest on record!) wore on.

I should probably also apologize to all the people who are waiting for thank-you letters for the holiday gifts we received. These gifts have certainly done quite a bit to bring our family closer together than ever, especially now that we have to share house space with the 4,382,573 pieces of new toys you've given to our children. Unfortunately, toy makers now make toys that share two common features:

1. They have a minimum of 173 moving and removable parts small enough for the baby to choke on.

2. They can survive a nuclear holocaust.

Despite our kids' best efforts, they only succeeded in breaking about a fourth of the toys before the end of Christmas day. Thus my son is now the proud dispatcher of the largest privately-owned fleet of teeny vehicles in the Free World while his sisters received enough doll accessories to outfit a miniature Princess Di and enough matching shoes to turn a Kardashian green with envy. My only consolation is that they form a carpet which will certainly thwart any midnight burglar—assuming that said burglar is attempting to cross our floor barefoot in the dark as I usually am. (Hopefully, the burglar will not use the words I usually do…)

While I'm on a roll, I also need to apologize to my family, my greatest source of writing inspiration. The 8-year-old was going to write a rebuttal column in which she points out all the stupid things I do, but she said that it would be too long, plus she needs me to keep this job because she has to think about us paying her college expenses eventually.

To the Hub, who spends most of his time worrying about the libel suit which may bankrupt us, and to everyone I've offended this year, I offer condolences and this promise. For the new year, I will attempt the following:

1. I'll try to call my children by their own names, or at least by names that might have originated on this planet and/or are not currently assigned to one of our pets.

2. I'll boycott all toys that have more than one moving part and all clothes that are dry-clean only. (If you see kids dressed in towels and playing with one Tinkertoy, send them home to me for lunch.)

3. I'll try to remember that God must have a great sense of humor, because there is no other possible explanation for election-year politicians and 3-year-olds.

4. I will say very, very nice things about anyone who is at all likely to carry a gun or a wrench.

5. I'll never, ever mention New Jersey. Seriously. Never.

6. I'll really try to send thank-you letters within the same century as the gift without telling the giver my real opinion of their piss-awful gifting choices, or suggesting they must have done their Christmas shopping after hitting the drinks limit at the pub, or out of revenge for that teddy I gave their kid last year—the one who sang "*It's a small world after all*" with no visible off-button (on the teddy). Well, then on the kid too. Mwahahah. *(C'mon. It was a little funny.)*

Another editorial comment from the Hub: *What's a thank-you note?*

❖ ❖ ❖

Chapter 36: Wait… What Are We Thankful For Again?

(Another blast from the past, adapted from column in Champaign Urbana News-Gazette, November, 1991)

◆ ◆ ◆

The Middle East? The economy? National health coverage? Blue or Red state? How to cook the perfect turkey?

Guess which question is on the minds of the 248,709,873 Americans preparing to shred 535 million pounds of turkey this Thanksgiving Day. (Actually, 248,709,872 Americans — my 7-year-old prefers peanut butter and jelly sandwiches.)

> *My 7-year-old's homemade turkey joke: Q. Which side of a turkey has the most feathers? A. The outside.*

It's no surprise that modern cooks are confused about turkeys. In 1621 our pilgrim forefathers, after surviving starvation and disease, not to mention fear of witches, Native Americans, and our pilgrim foremothers, crawled out of their pilgrim forehuts and stood around making gobbling noises.

To local turkeys, these irresistible noises said, "Hey, sailor, new in town?"

Our pilgrim forefathers promptly invented Thanksgiving. Every year after that, Americans would go outside, make gobbling noises, and bring home a turkey. But there have been changes since those pilgrim forebirds. Modern turkeys are naked, frozen, keep their bodily organs in plastic baggies, and are (after years of scientific breeding at the Dolly Parton Research Institute)

95% breast meat.

They are also so much larger that Americans who make the traditional gobbling noises are actually trying to say, "I have just suffered serious physical damage from lifting that sucker and I don't think I'll be able to have children."

My 9-year-old: Q. How do you tell a turkey from an elephant? A. If you don't know, I'm not eating Thanksgiving dinner at your house.

HOW TO FIX THE PERFECT TURKEY

Americans attach too much importance to Thanksgiving turkey. After all, even if you do blow the main dish of the single, most important meal of the year, and are branded a pathetic, incompetent failure in front of your in-laws, family, and friends, the dog will still love you. Probably. If she gets the scraps.

"But Barb," you protest, "surely there is A Better Way." To you Norman Rockwell wannabes I say, "Marge Klindera." Marge is a supervisor for the 45 turkey mavens at the Butterball Turkey Talk Line. They ministered to over 220,000 cases of turkey-trauma last year, 6600 on T-Day alone, from desperate chefs who wanted to know:

- What if you live in Seattle and on Thanksgiving day yours is one of 20,000 homes where the power goes out during peak roasting hours? *(And what if someone–we're not naming names, but he'll be on sofa sentry until next Thanksgiving—forgot to turn off the grill last time and the propane is all gone? Time for the traditional Thanksgiving bonfire. All those booklets from the power company pointing out that your neighbors are much better at saving energy than you will make excellent fuel. For that festive yet personalized touch, I hear Martha Stewart Online has instructions for making a homemade burnable effigy of power company executives.)*

- What if you forget you've put Tom in the bathtub to defrost and all of a sudden you notice you're showering with the main course? (*This little secret is between you and Tom, and I don't think he's going to tell.)*

- What if you've cooked the turkey in its plastic wrapper and you wonder if those blue and yellow markings on its skin are edible? *(Marge seems like a very nice person. I really don't think she makes this stuff up...)*

- What if you can't find the neck cavity for stuffing because you've never had a relationship with a turkey who wasn't past tense, so you're not sure exactly which opening represented his neck when he was present tense?

- And finally—my personal favorite—what if your kitten crawls into the turkey and falls asleep, and then just as you're about to pop it in the oven you notice a long furry tail hanging out which you're pretty sure is not standard-issue turkey equipment?

Marge was also happy to tell me the easiest way to fix turkey:

1. Make stuffing. There are only two ways to make stuffing; your mother's way and ~~your mother-in-law's way~~ the wrong way.

2. If you don't remove the little plastic bag of giblets before cooking, your turkey will not be ruined. Your family, however, will be physically incapable of saying the word 'Thanksgiving' without mentioning this incident. (*"Remember the time back in '91 when Great-Great-Grandma cooked the plastic bag inside the turkey?" "Yeah, that was pretty funny. Um... what's a turkey?" "I dunno... What's a Grandma?"*)

3. Rub skin with vegetable oil and place turkey on a flat rack. Cook at 325 degrees-F until golden brown, tenting the breast area with foil to keep it from drying out. Turkey is done when a meat thermometer says 180-185 degrees-F, NOT when your husband says the guests are going to start eating the piano if they don't get some dinner soon.

"But you don't want to overcook it as it could become dry, tough, and shredded when carved," advises Marge. (Come on, Marge — how could it be Thanksgiving without the traditional turkey shreds?)

MORE HOMEMADE TURKEY JOKES

My 7-year-old: Q. What do you get when you cross a turkey with an octopus? A. Finally, enough drumsticks to go around.

My 5-year-old: Q. Why did the turkey cross the road? A. It was the chicken's day off.

❖ ❖ ❖

Chapter 37: Yes, Barb, There Is

We don't see the inside of the mall very often. In fact, for years my children believed the North Pole was located halfway between Macy's and Sears, because Santa was there as often as they were.

But last week it was December, and I was standing in line in the middle of the mall so my kids could talk to a complete stranger in a red suit. There's not much to do while you wait your turn for the elves to extort $21.95 for photographic documentation of your terrified kid on Santa's lap. You could think back on all your carefully-chosen lessons and warnings about stranger-danger. But the fact is, if gangs of red-suited, white-bearded men were to pillage, loot, and generally lay waste to the whole town, our children would crawl out from the smoking ruins and call after them, "And a new GameBoy™ and Roller Blades and.."

So I began to study my fellow shoppers. There seemed to be two species of mall rats this time of year.

Shopper #1. Those who finished their shopping early and are only in the stores because they think it might be nice to replace their old Christmas tablecloth and centerpiece.

Shopper #2. Those who wouldn't know a Christmas table cloth if it wore mistletoe and sang "*Rudolph*" because since the Reagan Administration their dining room table has been buried under piles of wrapping paper, sewing, and craft projects. Shopper #1s may think that they are anonymous, but we #2s know better. #1s are the ones who got to the mall early enough to get parking places in the same state as the stores. They bought Baby Upchuck while stores still had their choice of foods for her to regurgitate, and Bucket-o-Yucko before they ran out of the neon slime.

But you #1s aren't fooling us by talking about how much you still have to do. We know who you are and we're sending a full list of your names and phone numbers to every PTA in town. By this time tomorrow, your houses will be surrounded by crack SWAT teams of Room Mothers with bull-horns: "This is your last warning. Come out with 3-dozen homemade cookies for the fourth-grade's holiday party and a hot dish for the teachers' luncheon or we'll hold a committee meeting out here and appoint you Chairperson of the Winter Carnival."

When I was a child, Christmas was easier. I only had three jobs to do. First came the annual Battle of the trees:

MY FATHER: "The traditional time to purchase a Christmas tree is the last minute on Christmas eve when the sellers give you their traditional price cuts."

US KIDS: "But Daddy, everyone else gets their Christmas tree the day after Thanksgiving."

MY MOTHER: "Why don't we get an artificial tree this year, maybe one of those pastel ones in colors that would amaze Frosty? And instead of our usual collection of chipped, homemade, mismatched ornaments and all that tinsel that clogs the vacuum, we could just hang blue balls with matching strings of blue lights."

US KIDS: "Uh, Daddy, about that Christmas Eve tree? Let's try for one with branches on at least one side this year."

My second Christmas job was buying presents. With nine brothers and sisters, we had to be creative: "Okay, I'll give her the bubbles and you can give her the bubble wand."

But my hardest Christmas job was going to see Santa. It wasn't that I didn't want to go. It was just that in the terror of finding myself on his knee I knew that I would never remember to tell him what I really wanted.

One year, I tried everything: writing down "Miss Mimi Poodle with the glitter collar", repeating it over and over while I waited in line, telling my sisters to remind me, even cutting the picture out of the *Sears Holiday Wish Book*. But it was no use. Santa always stumped me with his first question, "Have you been a good girl this year?" I always wanted to say, "Aren't you already supposed to know that? Haven't you been making a list and checking it twice?"

But I was worried that he did have the list, and this was a trick to see if I was willing to cop to that incident involving my younger sister's hair and our new safety will-not-cut-skin scissors.

ME: "Uh…"

SANTA: "How about a dolly?"

ME: "Uh…"

SANTA: "Ho, ho, ho! Next…"

I couldn't believe I had blown it. Santa was bringing me a dolly.

And to make matters worse, my neighbor Terry had been whispering heresy about Santa himself. I was desperate enough to turn to my older brother. We decided to approach the matter scientifically—wait for everyone to go to bed, and then get up and keep watch.

Next thing I knew, he was shaking me awake and telling me it was morning. "But don't worry," he assured me. He said he had been awakened by the sound of sleigh bells, and had tiptoed into the living room in time to see Santa heading back up the chimney.

I raced out and there, her collar glittering in the glow of the mismatched lights and the tinsel hiding most of tree's bare patches, stood Miss Mimi Poodle.

But it was years before I realized the best gift I got that year came from my big brother, and it wasn't the little red ball he gave me to go with the set of jacks from my sister.

❖ ❖ ❖

Chapter 38: It's A Wonderful Life. Or Not.

During Christmas at my house, everyone has a job:

• My husband is on Energy Patrol. In honor of the holidays, he adds a festive "Who-left-this-tree-plugged-in?" to his usual refrain of "Who-left-these-lights-on-close-that-door-were-you-born-in-a-barn?"

• The dog is on United Parcel Service Patrol. She greets UPS men with the same delight most people reserve for IRS audits and street mimes. It's risky to attempt to follow whatever the dog uses in place of thought processes, but we think she's decided UPS men make us move. I guess she figures that once we accumulate enough cardboard boxes, we're outa here. If we thwart her desire for UPS steak tartare, the dog usually sulks into my daughter's bedroom with its full-length mirror. There she gets another shock. Not only have we let in the boxes–we got a replacement dog too! Faced with universal betrayal, a human might despair. But our dog, the pinnacle of eons of canine evolution, knows all she has to do is mark her territory. On the bedroom carpet. Take that, and *that*, and WTH–that over there too–you encroaching UPS and ersatz dog wannabes.

• My daughters are on Santa Patrol. As the foremost authorities on Santa-related issues this side of the North Pole, their task is to explain Christmas to their younger brother.

Him: "How will Santa get in if we don't have a fireplace?"

Sisters: "Mrs. Santa irons him flat and he slides under the door. Then she has a special bicycle pump and she puffs him back up when he gets back."

* I'm on Better-Homes-&-Garden Patrol. My goal used to be to create a magazine Christmas: children in matching red plaid robes and pajamas are hanging up their red plaid stockings. On the red plaid sofa sit Mom and Dad in their matching red plaid hand-knit sweaters, sipping their red plaid eggnog, a red plaid spaniel at their feet. (*How to tell this picture is NOT Barb's family? Hint #1: all limbs (and heads) are actually in the frame. Hint #2: no hands are miming devil horns, gripping privates, or inserted in bodily orifices.*)

Reality? At bedtime on Christmas Eve in our house, we're lucky to find all the kids, let alone red plaid. Anyway, what Mom and Dad need right then is something more than eggnog. (Hot buttered industrial-strength Valium toddies comes to mind.)

Suddenly the doorbell rings for a holiday package delivery. The UPS Patrol goes ballistic, vowing to take no prisoners. The seven-year-old races for her bedroom, screaming, "Cover the mirror!" while the rest of the Santa Patrol tries to wrestle the package away from 65 pounds of enraged Border Collie. The Energy Patrol shouts,,"Close-that-door-we-don't-need-to-heat-the-whole-town!" while the BH&G Patrol recalculates our homeowners' liability coverage.

I start thinking about George Bailey, the Jimmy Stewart character in *It's a Wonderful Life*. "What would happen to Christmas around this place," I ask the dog, "If I wasn't here?" She gives me the intense Border Collie stare that seems to say, *"At least you wouldn't be having conversations with a dog who, on the intelligence scale of life, ranks right up there with dryer lint and Senate Confirmation Hearings."*

Just then, I hear a knock on our back door. There stands a familiar figure. "I'm your guardian angel," he says.

"You look a lot like Dan Quayle."

"Well, yes," he admits. "Things were slow between election years, so I took this extra job over the holidays."

"I thought the recession was over?"

"Technically. I believe we are on an irreversible trend toward more freedom and democracy—but that could change. If we do not succeed, then we run the risk of failure."

"You're Dan Quayle, all right," I agree. "So how do I find out what

Christmas would be like at our house if I wasn't around?"

Suddenly I'm back inside my house. Every surface is covered with mauve and teal decorations hung with miles of natural evergreen roping. With difficulty, I recognize the bare dining room table (which has been buried under my Christmas projects since the Fourth of July) and the family sitting around it. "We're so lucky that the fashion model Dad married after Mom disappeared is a gourmet cook," say the children cheerfully eating their vegetables.

"Yes, and I'm glad that my new wife Tiffanie's latest novel was a best-seller so we could spend the rest of the holidays skiing the Alps," agrees their father. The dog looks up from a floor littered with shredded UPS uniforms and burps happily.

"You call that Christmas?" I yell at them as they dig into their okra *en croute*. "I'm sorry, Mr. Quayle, but I've got to go back. Someone has to show them what Christmas is really about: stress, long lines, mismatched ornaments, the 197th rendition of *"We three kings of orient are, trying to smoke a rubber cigar, it was loaded, it exploded, blew us to yonder star"*, homemade gifts, kids waking up at O'dark:thirty to see if Santa's been there yet, the five-year-old saying, "I LOVE Christmas, but next year what I really want…"

As Mr. Quayle speeds off in his [non-carbon-neutral] limo, a hand waves to me and a voice floats back, "We'll let the sunshine in and shine on us, because today we're happy and tomorrow we'll be even happier."

It's a wonderful life.

◆ ◆ ◆

Chapter 39: Halloween Tips From A Bad Mother

I love Halloween. And by that I mean, of course, I love the excuse to buy giant bags of Hershey and Nestle candy bars, and not in those little wuss sizes either. Cause I'm ALL about the kids.

But when we moved to Scotland a few years ago, I wasn't sure how Halloween would work. So I consulted the brain trust: unsuspecting strangers who talk to me at the park. No, I know what you're thinking. It's the UK. When you see someone you know, you're required to turn around and walk immediately in the other direction on the off-chance they might want to talk to you. It has absolutely nothing to do with whether or not you like each other. You probably do. But that still doesn't mean you can talk in anywhere in public except for a pub.

The one exception to that rule is my secret weapon: my little dog. There is absolutely no card-carrying resident of the British Isles who won't stop to tell me that she's a fine wee doggie. And then they're mine for as long as it takes me to ask my question.

So this week I asked them about local Halloween customs. To my surprise, I found that the local tradition of "guising" (as in *dis*-guise) predates American trick-or-treat. Children dressed as witches or ghouls are expected to recite some song or poem in return for treats and money. Excellent.

Only... I'm just not sure I have enough chocolate for every kilt and child in Glasgow. So whilst (you get to say whilst here) my fine wee doggie and I are off buying more Hershey and Nestle Cadbury, I'll reblog last year's Halloween column below. (Clearly, I haven't gotten any better at this whole mothering thing in the interim...)

❖ ❖ ❖

I used to be a good mother.

Before the birth of my first child, I read thirty-seven instruction manuals warning of her possible future as an ax-murderer or Republican if I failed to diaper, dress, or dose her with natural fibers. I followed their instructions until that fateful day early in her second year when my husband took her into Chez Mac's to escape the rain. By the time I got there, it was too late. He bought her an ice-cream cone and she was having a spiritual experience. Through the chocolate, I could see her thinking, "This stuff was out there and I've been eating *yams*?"

It was all downhill from there. Of course, I tried to keep up appearances. But the problem was that although my kids hadn't read my Raising-the-Macrobiotic-Whole-Child manuals, each of them carefully studied the cultural treatises known as commercial advertising. Results?

- While I bought whole grain flours to bake macrobiotic breads so dense they weighed more than bricks and doubled very usefully as doorstops, my children insisted on eating only store-bought white bread. (In national taste-tests, consumers preferred Kleenex™.)

- While I bought natural fiber fabrics to sew their nonsexist playwear, my daughters insisted on wearing their girl-colored Better-Living-Through-Chemistry dresses to their tea parties, and my son refused to appear without his plastic superhero cape.

- While I bought developmental, non-gender-specific playthings, my daughters held fashion shows for the stuffed toys and dolls, and their brother built the blocks and Legos into weapons of mass doll-destruction.

I asked myself, "If my children are fed, dressed, and entertained by a bunch of men on Madison Avenue, how come none of those guys are ever around when a table, toilet, or tush needs to be swabbed?"

> *Mothering tip: talking to yourself is a common side-effect of motherhood. Generally speaking, bystanders will be more comfortable if you buy a small dog and pretend to address all comments to it while in public. (You should be concerned, though, when you start getting answers.)*

Luckily, there are two occasions in our child's year where the compulsive guilt-driven mother gets the chance to really go all out: birthdays and Halloween. For example, angst-Mom will spend several months and the better part of her life savings on birthday activities which her child's guests complete in two and a half minutes, ignore, or throw up on.

On Halloween, angst-Mom (who refuses to spend $15 on a cheap plastic Miss America or armed turtle costume) will cheerfully spend the week's food budget on fabric and sew non-stop for days to create adorable little animal costumes.

As a maternal veteran of ten Halloweens and seventy-six costumes [each of the four kids has at least two costumes per year–the adorable one I create and the one they actually wear], I would like to offer the following Halloween tips:

- You can justify spending a small fortune on the costume by telling yourself that your child or your child's sibling will wear it next year. (This will be easy for most women, who have at the back of their closets a number of bridesmaids dresses which they were supposed to "cut off and wear to parties later." That will happen in the same fantasy where those animal costumes get re-worn.)

- If you have been attempting to raise an egalitarian, non-sexist child using any means other than extensive genetic engineering, Halloween is the time to admit total defeat. I was driving a group of eight and nine-year-olds on a field trip before Halloween and asked about their costume plans. "I'm going to be a fairy/butterfly/princess," said the girls. "I'm going to be a ninja carrying a star with blood and guts and an eyeball on it/ a guy escaped from a toxic waste dump after all his skin is peeled off/ zombie," said the boys.

- Five minutes before the school Halloween parade when your kids refuse to be caught dead in the little animal costumes, you can make a great ninja-turtle-shell with a garbage can lid, and your best silk bathrobe will do for Miss America.

◆ ◆ ◆

Chapter 40: Valentine's Day BC (BEFORE Children) vs AD (AFTER Delivery)

In the years before children (BC) I considered myself a reasonably cultured person.

- <u>Books?</u> I bought them in hardbound editions so I'd be early enough to disagree with the review in the *New York Times*.

- <u>Movies?</u> I saw them before Siskel & Ebert. *(Barb's Guide to Films: if the characters kiss a lot, have sex, and then kill each other, it's American. If the characters smoke a lot, have sex, and then kill themselves, it's foreign.)*

- <u>Music?</u> I once sat through an entire performance of *Nixon in China*. On purpose.

- <u>Food?</u> I ate pasta before they stopped calling it spaghetti. Even before you could get squid-ink pasta with arugula oil at the Piggly Wiggly.

- <u>News and Current Events?</u> I cared about who won the Booker Prize. Really.

But in the years AD (after delivery) things changed.

- <u>Books?</u> After spending three hours in the children's section of the library picking out 47 titles in the *"Shelley's Sleepover Surprise"* series for my daughters and another 35 of *"Sammy Skunk Surprises Shelley"* for my son, I only have time to grab whatever adult library books haven't yet been re-shelved as I'm checking out. Some titles I totally did not make up: *Do It Yourself Coffin for Pets, Snow Caves for Fun and Survival, 101 Uses for a Dead Cat* (Actually, this last one was useful—we've had lots of cats.)

• Movies? If it didn't feature an animated rodent, I didn't see it.

• Music? I'd sing "*Shake, shake, shake my sillies out*" along with the Raffi playlist. Then I'd realize two things. I knew all the words. And I was only one in the car.

• Food? We favored restaurants where the paper-wrapped entrees came boxed with a plastic surprise. Occasionally we scored a babysitter (preferably someone new in town who hadn't heard about that incident involving the four-year-old, the banana, sixteen metal miniature cars, and the microwave) and we went to a restaurant with cassoulet and candles instead of children and ketchup. But I still had an uncontrollable urge to grab a stack of napkins 'just in case' and to cut up somebody's meat. And I couldn't shake the feeling that I had to eat fast because when the food arrived, somebody would announce that they hafta go *right now*.

• News? Luckily not much happened from mid-80's to mid-90's. Until the Gulf War, I only turned on the news to find out which day it was so I wouldn't miss trash pickup again. Of course, in 1989 I did have to tune in for the Collapse of Godless Communism and the Triumph of Western Ideals of Freedom, Capitalism, and Fast Food Franchises. And the Kennedy rape trial.

With the departure of Child#4, I've now graduated from AD to LBWKLH&DD**.

**(A priest, a minister and a rabbi were talking about when life begins. The priest said: "Life begins at conception." The minister said: "Life begins when the fetus is viable." The rabbi said: "*L*ife *b*egins *w*hen the *k*ids *l*eave *h*ome and the *d*og *d*ies.")*

Books and Music? Thanks to e-book readers and noise-cancelling headphones, I can now sit on public transportation and nobody can tell I'm actually reading *Debby & the Duke do Dallas* while listening to Gretchen Wilson's *Redneck Woman*, (although I get some odd looks when I belt the "*Hell, Yeah's*" out loud…)

Movies? Playing catch-up. Apparently some movies in the 80s and 90s did *not* have animated rodents. Who knew?

Food? I live in England. I can only dream of In-N-Out Burgers…

<u>News?</u> Thanks to Twitter, I'm on it. #trending, #Kate Middleton, #babybump

Of course, the one day of the year that really separates the BCs, the ADs, and the LBWKLH&DDs is Valentine's Day. From the recession, I know that eating in is the new eating out. From watching Hallmark commercials, I know that Mr. BC arrives with flowers, candy and a card expressing his deepest thoughts in rhyming couplets. And from reading Cosmo in the grocery store checkout lines, I know that Ms. BC, wearing some X-rated lingerie, shows him into the dining room where they share an intimate candlelit supper pour deux. (Whipped cream optional).

Yes, readers, the real dividing line between BC, AD, and LBWKLH&DDs is: the dining room. BCs have one. ADs have a room which was described by the Realtor as a formal dining room, but which has not been the site of an actual meal since Thanksgiving of 1987.

As an AD, I didn't want the other moms to think I was sacrificing my children's self-expression and creativity on the altar of crass commercialism by having them send out pre-Hallmarked Garfield valentines with little candies attached. So each year I excavated the dining room table from under the sewing machine and a few dozen of my current sewing and quilting projects. Then I re-covered the table with enough art supplies for my kids to make valentines for every child in a three-state radius. After days of creative self-expression, each child would have turned out one masterpiece such as:

Roses are red, violets are pink.
Mom makes me send cards to the whole class,
But you still stink.

(Cue the late-night run for whatever candy-clad valentines were still left in the stores.)

But I'm ready for this Valentine's Day. When my husband arrives and asks, "Hey, this wasn't one of those holidays where I have to DO something, was it?", I will strike a sultry pose in my *Life's too short to stuff mushrooms* apron, and hand him his valentine:

Roses are red, some violets are white.
Let's do something wild, spontaneous and different RIGHT ON THE DINING
ROOM TABLE.
Let's eat there tonight.

◆ ◆ ◆

Chapter 41: Revenge.

Have you received the traditional Christmas email from relatives and friends telling you how incredibly wonderful that past year has been for them?

Right. That's why I don't send them out either.

But maybe it's time we got even. I've created a newsy, personal, generic form email letter. Simply send me the names of your family and your street address, and I'll insert them into the following letter template.

◆ ◆ ◆

Dear (check one)

___Unidentified Person Who Sent Us a Christmas Letter Last Year*. (*Even though we could never figure out who you were, but your letter said you were obviously so wildly successful we may want to borrow money from you soon.)

___Loving Family and Friends**. (**As you can see from the following letter, we are wildly successful ourselves this year but we won't lend you any money so don't even ask.)

The fabulously successful Karpenagle family here at the impressive Karpenagle house on Maple Street in Champaign, Illinois, want to wish you a traditional Karpenagle Happy Holidays and New Year. (Not that you could possibly be as merry and happy as we are, of course, but you should never give up hope. Even if the new episodes of The Walking Dead and a winning lottery ticket are the only hope you have for the *coming year...)*

This year Myra Sue Karpenagle has been balancing her careers as nuclear physicist, fashion model, and mother of four. Her latest redecorating of the tasteful Karpenagle house here on Maple Street in Champaign, IL has been featured in several design magazines, while her selfless volunteer work on behalf of blind baby whales has won her the coveted Champaign, IL PTA Mother-of-the-Year award.

Wally Karpenagle has been promoted. Again. In his new position, he provides important policy advice to God. In his free time, he coached the little Melvin Karpenagle soccer team to its third consecutive World Championship. He also produced enough zucchini in the Karpenagle garden to feed several Third World countries, and published his cookbook, *"1001 Things You Never Guessed You Could Do With a Zucchini"*, which made the best-seller lists for three months in a row.

Young Wally Jr. Karpenagle is still doing well at the university. As captain, he led their football team to an unprecedented winning season while, of course, maintaining the straight-A average that has just won him a full scholarship to Harvard Medical School and an appearance on the "Wheel of Fortune".

Luella Karpenagle has been enjoying her year abroad as a Rhodes Scholar. Her pathbreaking article on the sex life of newts was published in an actual scientific journal and she is negotiating with several major studios for the film rights.

Baby Fionella Karpenagle has, at 9 ½ months, begun talking in full sentences (Russian, French, and English) and is writing novels on the new iPoop Baby Genius tablet. Yesterday she toddled over to the piano and picked out a Mozart concerto, the Goldberg Variations, and an original overture.

Espotté, the impressive Karpenagel dog, was named Best of Show and Best of Breed on Earth. He was also featured in a recent "60 Minutes" report for his controversial attempts to keep the impressive Karpenagle house on Maple Street safe from the growing numbers of French poodles with silly haircuts in Champaign, Il.

We are enclosing some candid shots of the impressive Karpenagle family with friends. (President Obama is the one on the left, behind the Duke and Duchess of Cambridge, and the Pope is the one with the little round hat.)

We in the Karpenagel family in the impressive house here on Maple

Street in Champaign, Illinois hope we have served as an inspiration to you.

Love, Myra Sue, Wally, Wally Jr, Luella, Melvin, Fionella and Espotté Karpenagle

❖ ❖ ❖

Actually, I only send out Christmas letters myself if we have moved recently and people will need the correct address to send gifts and money. This seems, in fact, to be a trend. So far, the only one in our house who has received a Christmas letter is the dog. Of course, she did send out a dynamite Christmas letter last year.

❖ ❖ ❖

PART 5: TRAVEL

♦ ♦ ♦

Chapter 42: My Old Man And The Car

With my father's birthday coming up this week, I've found myself thinking about the role cars have played in defining our relationship. Feeling it was important to be close to my mother at such a time, I arranged to be born at Columbus Hospital on the north side of Chicago, where she was currently in labor. But my father missed my big debut. He was trapped in his car on the South Side while the Museum of Science and Industry hauled a German submarine across Lake Shore Drive. I think he and Das Boat bonded in those special moments, though, and he's been back often to visit it.

After we moved to California, my father's driving followed only two rules. The first was NEVER BRAKE, particularly if the road was steep and winding. "You don't want to wear out the brake shoes," he remark to relatives visiting from the flatlands. They would nod, their white knuckles gripping the seats while their lives flashed before their eyes. Ignoring the spectacular scenery zipping by at near-light speed, we kids fought over who got to sit next to the windows and have some slight chance to leap out of the car before it plunged over the next cliff.

My father's other rule was to say the rosary every time we went farther than the corner. Since he had a habit of turning around and watching us as we stumbled through our "Hail Marys" in the back seat, these trips contained some of my most deeply moving religious experiences. "A nun, God," I'd bargain. "I'll enter the convent if you make my father look at the road."

My father takes the next curve, tires squealing and cigar smoke drifting over his shoulder.

I sweeten the deal. "And if you get him to use the brake, God, you can

133

have a few of my sisters too."

With so many kids, my parents must have suffered from memory loss. It's the only explanation for the way they kept trying to take vacations which involved driving through Nebraska. (State motto: *"We're in your way."*) At first it just meant the obligatory ticket, since it's apparently against Nebraska state law to have out-of-state plates. Then came the year my parents decided to save on motels by hitching a pop-up camper behind the Vomit Comet. Our fellow campers were astonished at the speed with which we kids set it up at night. They didn't know my parents wouldn't let anyone go to the bathroom until it was done.

Things went pretty well on the trip east from California:

- *DAY 1, The Sierra Mountains.* MY PARENTS: "Isn't that beautiful?" US KIDS: "Where?"

- *DAY 2, The Rocky Mountains.* MY PARENTS: "Isn't that beautiful?" US KIDS: "Where?"

- *DAY 3, Nebraska.* MY PARENTS: "Is there a problem, officer?" MY LITTLE BROTHER: "Are you going to shoot all of us or just my dad?"

Then came the return trip. My parents didn't believe in throwing away their money on fancy automotive 'options'—like car radios—whose sole purpose was to separate rich people from their cash. So we didn't know about the tornado in Nebraska until the trailer headed for Oz, pulling the car with it. Luckily, just as one sister swore she saw a witch on a bicycle and some cows fly past, the hitch popped off when the pop-up pooped out.

We resumed the trip, sans trailer, with nine kids layered into the twelve inches of space between the sleeping bags and the roof. After driving through the desert for hours without seeing another vehicle, we came upon a young couple stranded by their broken car. But when my dad offered them a lift, they took one look and said they'd wait for the next car. (For the rest of his life, my father often mentioned his worry about that young couple. I suspect they did the same.)

Our first landlords told us they didn't believe in selling any real estate they'd acquired. My father felt the same way abut his cars. "There's nothing wrong with that perfectly good car," he would insist as he towed Gus, our geriatric VW, home for the fifth time that week. "You must have done something to it."

He still blames me for the demise of 2o+ year-old Perfectly Good Gus. I called for TAPS when the last working gear froze solid in the on-lane entrance to Santa Cruz beach one hot Saturday afternoon. The ensuing traffic jam—

legendary even by California standards—made the evening news and lasted until a carful of frustrated surfers picked up Gus and moved him to the side of the road.

I had my 15-minutes of unwanted fame.

Gus became a VW parts organ donor.

My father never quite got over the loss.

❖ ❖ ❖

Chapter 43: My Editor Was So Wrong....

Back in my journalist days, I wrote a column for a chain of newspapers. But my editor was the one who chose the headlines, and for this one he penned: *"Years from now, this vacation will only be a fond memory..."*

Well, since that was in 1991, I think this qualifies for the "years from now" part. I'm still waiting for the fond memories.

◆ ◆ ◆

I hate vacationing.

Sure, it always starts well. We rise with the dawn! We go back to sleep, because seriously? Dawn?

Hours later, we roll onto the freeway for the 400-mile trip which is supposed to take about six hours—if you bring an empty Coke can for each passenger's use. Six hours and less than a hundred miles later, we are in a parking lot which the map had optimistically listed as Interstate-94 out of Illinois.

On our trips we each have defined roles: Driver, Gasper, Barfer, Asker, Bladder, Belly, and Barker. The Driver's job is to give the Gasper something to do. The Asker's job is to inquire, "Are we there yet?" at least 137 times an hour. The Barfer, Bladder, and Belly's roles are obvious after the first mile or so:

- *"Is that a McDonalds? I'm hungry."*

- *"You know what I didn't havta do before we left? Well, I hafta do it. RIGHT NOW."*

- *"And the dog's farting really bad."*

- *"And I'm hungry. And I think I'm gonna barf."*

The Barker lets passing motorcyclists know this vehicle is protected by an Anti-Motorcycle Attack Border Collie. I don't know what motorcyclists think of sixty-plus pounds of hysterically yelping Border Collie plastering our car windows with Border Collie excretions. But I do know the Driver spends a lot of time informing us about the netherworld conditions which will have to prevail before the Barker takes another trip with him.

Ever anxious for educational opportunities, the Driver decides to get a closer look at the trail bike mounted behind the car in front of us. Hearing the Gasper, he points out that there are still several atoms of space between our bumpers. "I bet they have one of those new indexed shifters," he says. "See those two little buttons on the hand brakes?"

"No." The Gasper (guess who?) well...gasps. "But if you pull up any more, we'll be in their back seat and I can ask them about it."

We arrive in Michigan to discover they've been having a drought here for months. So I'm not surprised when it begins to rain. Although it often takes buying a non-refundable airline ticket, sometimes all I have to do to make it rain is pack a picnic basket.*

*[Case in point: last year, I visited my sister in California. Even though they were in the fourth year of a drought, I made it rain. She had seen rain before, but she was very pleased for her children's sake.]

By evening it clears up a bit, so we hit the beach.

4-year-old: "What is the name of this rock?"

Years from now, I think, *when he is a world-famous geologist, he'll look back to the moment when his mother started him on the path to his career.* Gently, I begin: "They call it sedimentary. See all the layers? That's because zillions of years ago...

4-year-old: "No, I think its name is Judy." The former geologist goes off to build a sand condo for Judy Rock.

We take a scenic hike to the scenic viewpoint in Sleeping Bear Dunes National Seashore. We know this is the right spot because there is a scenic bench at the top of a huge sand dune and a helpful National Park Service Mafia sign which actually says, "Scenic Viewpoint. Do not dig a hole and bury anyone in the Dunes." (The 4-year-old is clearly disappointed when his sister reads the sign to him. I think he'd been weighing the benefits of being an only child.)

At weeks' end, we leave the cottage to grab the last vacant campsite in the state of Michigan because the Driver thinks it's time to expose the kids to the Real Outdoors—whispering pines, smoke-scented air, babbling river, Grateful Dead fans with powerful car stereos, pit toilets. Actually, the air seems to be scented with whatever the Deadheads are smoking in the next campsite over. When the wind shifts, it's the pit toilet's turn.

Down at the river, most of the babbling comes from a group of eco-tourist canoes headed downstream. Their occupants are inexplicably dressed in polyester leopard-print loincloths and bone necklaces. The cavemen canoeists have evidently been hitting the pterodactyl juice because several of them turn over in about 18-inches of water. "Don't worry," one missing-link assures his fellows, "I can give you mouth-to-mouth recitation."

By morning, the Barker is almost comatose from exhaustion. You would be too if you had to spend all night guarding our campsite from marauding raccoons and our pit toilets from all those other campers. The Driver decides the kids have been exposed to enough in the Great Outdoors—I think he's referring to what the other campers did when our dog wouldn't allow them near our pit toilets—so we give up and head for home at last.

But we have to stop, because I'm showing symptoms of acute retail-withdrawal. Every store we pass starts to look good to me. Just as I'm lobbying seriously for the Antiques & Fresh Bait Shoppe, we come to the high point of my vacation—the Outlet Mall. A quick Visa-fix later and we're on the road again.

I love vacationing. Especially my favorite part—that moment when you finally know the family vacation is over.

[Falling to my knees and kissing the ground is optional.]

❖ ❖ ❖

Chapter 44: Over The Rivers & Through Chez Mac Drive-Thru We Go...

For all you amateurs out there planning a summer car trip with your children —we recommend at least three under age six—here are a few professional tips.

PACKING: Make two piles, Essential and Nonessential. The first thing to put in the Essential pile is several industrial-sized packages of diapers. You never know when you'll be in some foreign locale (anywhere it's a toll call to your pediatrician) where they might not have disposable diapers.

Also, your children will naturally want to bring several mementos of home. You can refuse them, at least the first couple of dozen times they ask. In the end, however, you'll find it's easier just to go ahead and add the Ms. Dolly, Miss Baby, and Mr. Ernie dolls, plus all the kids' bedding, clothes, books, toys, and electronic gadgets to the Essential pile.

This pile should also contain large stocks of snack foods with the average nutritional value of carpet lint. Relax! Only total strangers will actually see you feeding it to your kids, and the odds are they won't mention it to your in-laws. These snacks will allow you to drive for extended periods without stopping the car, sometimes 16 to 18 minutes at a stretch.

In the Nonessential pile, you can put the road maps and your clothes, if you want. But there won't be enough room in the car for them, so really...why bother? I advise slipping in a change of any underwear that will fit into that little pocket in the driver's door. Something unisex works well here.

LOADING: a key element is the vehicle itself. For the full roadtrip experience, we recommend something elderly and fairly decrepit. Speculation on your chances of actually arriving at your destination will provide endless hours of car conversation. Of course, your car will already contain the usual standard equipment—your car seats, strollers, diaper bags, and 3,478 plastic prizes given out by Chez Big Mac over the past 3 1/2 years.

Be sure you pack everything into *Teenage Mutant Ninja Turtle* and *My Little Pony* pillowcases. Not only do they stuff well into your car, they look particularly festive when the bellboy at your hotel loads them onto one of those little carts and parades after you across the lobby before the awed stares of your fellow guests.

TRAVELING: One parent is *The Driver*. He is responsible for the operation of the vehicle and for refusing to stop and ask directions even though it's been several hundred miles since the last recognizable road sign and the GPS shows your little vehicle icon surrounded by a field of black (or even worse, blue) as if you've driven off the edge of the known universe.

The other parent is *The Feeder*. Her job is to throw a steady stream of Chocolate Whizzies over her shoulder into the backseat—*TIP: Do NOT ever turn around to see what they are actually doing with these*—and also to ask The Driver if he is falling asleep.

Occasionally they switch places 'so he can get some rest'. This is not usually successful, however, as he will spend the entire rest time telling her not to hit that car or that fence. This is hardly fair because she has never actually hit anything. Okay, there was that incident with those trees, but they aimed for her so they deserved everything they got...

One of the high points of every family car trip is, of course, stopping at roadside restaurants. It is important to keep in mind that children love variety and will be delighted to stop at any interesting looking restaurant. Of course, they won't actually eat food in any establishment other than Chez Big Mac's.

The first ritual of restaurant stops involves parents begging kids to go to the bathroom. Several recent scientific studies, however, have offered conclusive proof that children's bladders can only be activated by the sight of hot food being placed in front of their parents.

Always leave a large tip. This ensures good will on your return visit, which may occur quite soon because about 125 miles down the road the four-year-old will announce that she left Ms. Dolly there, and it's okay if you don't go back— she'll just never sleep again.

ENTERTAINMENT: with the toys, books, movies, and electronica you brought, most children will entertain themselves beautifully for about the first half-mile. After this, you may want to consider some educational games to pass the time:

- Reading Readiness: Every child who is even nominally verbal can read Chez Big Mac signs. They will enjoy pointing every one of these out to you, assuring you that they are dying of hunger because they haven't eaten in minutes.

- Telling Time: In this game, the children ask every twelve seconds, "How long till we get there?" Some parentally correct replies: "Get where? We're not going anywhere, we're just out enjoying the scenic six-lane freeway." or "Why don't you see how many license plates you can find that match ours?"

- Math Skills: In this game, you count how many times The Driver refuses to stop before the six-year-old—who has eaten 138 Chocolate Whizzies—throws up. A rollicking variation of this involves speculation about whether the peculiarly luminous green of her face would really glow in the dark.

If you carefully prepare for your family car trip and follow all these tips, i'm sure you'll end up the way we usually do—staying home and settling for Big Macs and Chocolate Whizzies.

❖ ❖ ❖

PART 6: PETS

♦ ♦ ♦

Chapter 45: Life Begins When The Kids Leave Home And The Dog Dies

As proof of the continuing deterioration to be expected from advanced cases of parenthood, we decided it was time we acquired a puppy. Of course, before we got her we did careful research to determine the most intelligent and trainable breed for a family dog. Those who know how this technique has paid off for us in the past will not be surprised to learn that we became the proud owners of Natasha, a Border Collie who looked like Spuds McKenzie and boasted approximately two brain cells.

We reasoned that dog ownership would encourage the kids to spend time outdoors, become more responsible, and enjoy devoted companionship. Of course, the kids and the dog never got that memo. Instead I now got to spend healthful, responsible stretches of time in the great outdoors hanging around fences in my bathrobe and begging the dog to "go here".

We consulted several books about training your Border Collie. These related tales of dogs performing feats of genius and bravery that would make even the most hardened Lassie scriptwriter blush. "Dan," his master would say, "Go to Pennsylvania, cut my sheep, Fluffy, out of the flock of five million and get her home by dinner." Dan, who barked in complete sentences, probably did the shopping and dropped off the dry-cleaning along the way.

Another interesting concept of puppy training is the "pack leader". This theory says your dog will kick sand in your face and despise you for being a weenie if you don't immediately and firmly establish your position as head wolf. Of course, while the real wolf pack leader would rip the throat out of any wolf who didn't obey him, you are cautioned that any display of physical force on your part will cause your dog to grow up a terminal neurotic and, probably, an ax-murderer. In addition, Natasha developed a little condition the vet called submissive bladder, so nobody in their right mind would try to dominate her. At least, not more than once.

I have heard that some Border Collies are able to guard and herd their master's children. But I found out otherwise one winter day when I went to the bathroom. Of course, like all mothers, I did this with the door open to listen for sounds of carnage. If I had to close the door, it served as signal for every child and animal in a three-state radius to fling themselves against it, demanding to know exactly what I was doing in there and for how long I intended to do it. This particular time, I hadn't been in there more than 30-seconds before I looked out the window and saw the barefoot preschooler and puppy (with the keenly honed herding instincts of generations of championship breeding) running down the street in opposite directions. I was momentarily tempted to let them keep going, but we did actually pay quite a bit for the dog.

In earlier years, we sniggered with amused superiority over stories of friends and neighbors who had to remortgage the house in the face of canine calamity, such as doggie surgical teams called in to remove a $1,200 tennis ball from the stomach of the family mutt. Thus the Hub and I agreed we would never authorize the vet's use of extraordinary measures (costing more than $50) to prolong our ~~wallet's hemorrhage~~ dog's suffering. But all of this was forgotten the midnight I was awakened by the dog being spectacularly ill. To my horror, I saw her foaming at the mouth. With visions of rabies shots for the entire household, I rushed her to the vet, wondering how much cash I could raise quickly if we sold off a few extra children.

This was the point when I discovered that the dog we had chosen for her breed's intelligence had eaten every bar of soap in the house and was retching soapsuds.

Sorry to say, Natasha doesn't represent a fluke in my history of pet ownership, starting with our old college cat, Buster, who spent his days (when he wasn't having epileptic seizures) with his head up a lampshade. But for show-stopping density, the true champion was our cat, Cournot, who once stayed up in a tree for three days because she saw her reflection in an upstairs window and thought the other cat was after her. To our astonishment, she did prove to be an efficient mouser in our infested rental house. Our only theory was that as she was lying there with her mouth open, drooling, suicidal mice jumped in.

Sadly, the day came when we had to choose between the cat and our son, who turned out to be allergic to her. This was a difficult choice because while our son had never coughed up a hairball, he was not a very good mouser either. Also, the cat bathed herself, we had never had to change her diaper, and we didn't think she would expect us to pay for a college education.

I wrote out an ad – *"Young lady Persian Cat from good home seeks new family because son is allergic."* The phone rang day and night with people who were apparently desperate for a used cat. I'm not making this up. I don't know if there was something in my advertisement which was code for "free crack", but Madison Avenue should consider using sales pitches involving secondhand Persians.

"Yes, ladies and gentlemen, if you order this amazing cookware value today, we will include absolutely free this used Persian cat. Operators are standing by..."

❖ ❖ ❖

Chapter 46: Of Mice And Moms

Since my last pet column, I've had total strangers come up to me and completely seriously suggest we should have kept the cat and gotten rid of the allergic kids. They may have had a point.

Although I chose a good home for the ex-cat, I was still easy prey to the guilt visited on me by the 8-year-old whose cat I had just evicted. [NOTE: *Of course the 8-year-old also loved rodents. In her entire life, I doubted she'd seen more than three movies which didn't include animated rodents. And she loved every one of them, from Anatole, the bravest mouse in France, to Mickey, the richest mouse in pants.*]

The pet-store people were ready and waiting for us. We walked into the store and the adorable puppies on their newspapers in the front window reminded the 3-year-old of what he'd refused to take care of before we left but had to do RIGHT NOW. I asked how much the rodents cost and discovered they were practically free. So I left my daughter to pick out her almost-free rodent and took my son to the bathroom.

When I returned a few minutes later, the 8-year-old was standing by the cash register with a tiny boxed rodent in her hand and a Mona Lisa look of beatific delight on her face. Next to her was an enormous pile containing about $500 worth of rodent paraphernalia. The equally delighted rodent ~~pimp~~ ~~purveyor~~ re-homer explained she felt sure we would want to provide our new rodent with the basics which would ensure it continued the high quality of life it had come to expect in its pet-store residence.

- There was the palatial split-level abode including a complicated series of climbing tubes so we wouldn't have a claustrophobic rodent.

- There was about an 18-year supply of gourmet rodent chow, vitamins, and litter so we wouldn't have an unhealthy rodent.

- And of course, there were a variety of wheels, toys, and a little clear ball for excursions so we wouldn't have a bored rodent.

My husband suggested naming our new rodent "Chewy" in honor of the dog's strong interest in it, while I felt "Bubonic Plague" might add the correct note of historic panache. My daughter, of course, chose "S'mores", which I practically had to have insulin even to say.

For my daughter, it was instant love. She played endlessly with the rodent, and even—I'd have to sit down and put my head between my knees whenever I saw this—kissed it. For me, getting used to having a rodent on purpose seemed about as easy as getting used to breathing underwater. Luckily, the rodent appeared suicidally bent on escape from Rodent-Oz, so I figured we wouldn't be enjoying its company for much longer.

I'm not sure how S'mores got out so often. I suspect it got little chisels and saws smuggled inside its Vermin Chow. But as soon as an escape was spotted, the alarm would go out and we'd have to follow the trail of rodent droppings to its new hideout. This was complicated by the dog, who very diligently consumed all evidence of the rodent's passage. Once the rodent was spotted, of course, we had another problem—getting S'mores back into Rodent-Oz before being spotted by the dog.

That meant an adult had to pick up the rodent. Deliberately. But due to some mystical alignment of planets and luck, my husband was never around during one of The Great Escapes. (This didn't actually come as a surprise to anyone. We have four children, and not one of them has ever thrown up on the Hub. If I was out, they waited. It was almost a given that I could return any time, day or night, and someone would immediately barf on me...) Similarly, I swear that S'mores would wait until the Hub's plane had taken off before making another bid for freedom. And I would have to pick up a rodent.

Before becoming a parent, I was a reasonably fastidious person. Over the years, these standards had, under merciless siege (and much vomiting), disappeared. Only two elements remained—I didn't vote Republican and I didn't touch rodents. It became clear that at least one of my core principles would have to go.

You'll probably recognize me on election day. I'll be the one carrying the rodent.

❖ ❖ ❖

Chapter 47: Batwoman Rides Again

"You should get a cat," my neighbor said. I had just told him how a tiny mouse ran across the room directly over the dog's paws. The dog only yawned, obviously not considering rodents as part of her job description. Now if it had been an adorable baby bunny or whatever the dog was chewing on as the squirrels in the clematis above our doorway screamed bloody murder at her...

It's not as though we haven't had predatory pets, as this blog piece from a few years ago recalls...

◆ ◆ ◆

A couple of nights ago, I heard the cats get on their motorcycles in the middle of the night and start doing laps around the living room. The dog chased after, barking how Mom was going to catch them and then they would *really* be in trouble. They were knocking things over, crashing into the walls, and generally having one heck of a good time.

The next morning I woke up and they were all sitting by my bed with " *Cats rule and dogs drool*" grins on their faces. I was about to get out of bed when I noticed their looks of total concentration on where I was stepping. Sure enough, I was inches from squishing... a bat. Or, to be more specific—a cute, fuzzy, quite-recently-deceased ex-bat.

I stood on my bed for a while, yelling and generally trying to think of someone who could provide 5:30am bat-removal services. But all of my bat-removers were out of the state. Some of them were (wisely) out of the country. There was my father-in-law, but as he informed me, he'd just checked the fine print, and bat-removal was not in his retirement job description. So eventually, I put on latex gloves (several on each hand), grabbed some trash bags, and managed to entomb the bat in the garbage can. My gagging scared the dog, but the cats were clearly disgusted that I failed to appreciate their mighty bat-prowess.

That night at the neighborhood picnic, I was telling this story when people asked if I had the bat tested for rabies. One person told me a high percentage of the local bat population were carriers, and that I was a bad Kitty-Mom.

The Hub has often noted that neither of our cats was a candidate for Mensa (although he does feel they could play a role in scientific research). He pointed out it was unlikely a healthy bat would have come into the house, and inconceivable that our cats could catch it. I must admit the picture of a suicidal bat deciding to end it all by flapping into one of their mouths held a certain ring of truth.

So the following day I called the vet to see if I had to worry about the kittens. Next thing I knew, there was a Public Health doctor on the phone and she sounded excited. "I'm going to be your Case Manager. You have to get the bat out of the trash right away."

I said that it was 90°F outside and the bat had been cooking in that trashcan all day.

"Okay, get it out and put it in your freezer," she replied.

"Who is this really?" I said. "Is that you, Sarah?" (my boss)

After the doctor assured me she was a real doctor who was not named Sarah, and after I assured her that a dead, baked bat had zero chance of ending up in my freezer, we agreed I would fish the bat out of the trash and bring it to the Public Health department in the basement of a downtown hospital. "I'll have a police escort waiting for you," the doctor told me.

"Okay, Sarah, I know this is you."

But I went home, got the bat out of the trash, and put it into my picnic jug with lots of ice. The cats were very pleased I'd brought them back their bat, but then disappointed to discover I selfishly refused to share with them.

[Digression: at this point in the story, every man I've told this to asks what the bat looked like. The answer is that I may be a bad Kitty-Mom, but even if I had done horrible things like murder babies or vote Republican I would not have deserved to look at the former-bat, and so I did NOT remove it from its SAFEWAY "Ingredients for Life" plastic bag-shroud. You people need to get a life.]

I arrived at the hospital and walked up to the desk. "I have a bat."

They sprang into action. One receptionist pointed her finger at me. "Just stay right there. Don't move." The other one called for security and told them their bat had arrived. Then with two guards on either side of me—talking into their walkie-talkies so that they could alert everyone along the route that Rabies-Woman was stalking the hospital corridors—we made our way down to the Public Health lab.

After further bat-chitchat and discussion of the important bat-related Public Health Department responsibilities, I was allowed to leave. They presented me with the jug—minus the bat. I assured them it was now their jug, and I'd be buying my season's ski lift tickets in hell before that jug came back to my house.

A few days later, I got a call from the Public Health doctor, who told me my bat did NOT have rabies. She sounded quite sad about it. I told her I had learned my lesson, and if it ever happened again, I would know just what to do.

Sneak out behind my father-in-law's house and pitch that bat into his woods.

◆ ◆ ◆

PART 7: DEATH

❖ ❖ ❖

Chapter 48: The Day I Killed Mom—A (MOSTLY) True Story

When she turned fifty, my mother took up a new career: dying. It was a family tradition, she explained. "People in my family don't make it out of their fifties. So we have to be ready to go."

Each Christmas, she announced, would probably be her last—so no point in putting up a real tree or all that decorating. Her grandchildren would nod, and go right on dragging in and decorating a huge tree, around which our even more huge family would celebrate as usual, with Mother baking, making up beds, passing around Baileys Irish Cream, and loving every second of the noise and mess and confusion.

After pursuing dying for a few decades, it was time for her to think about retiring. But since there were really only two ways (ruling out vampires and/or zombies) to move on from that career choice—a coffin, or coming back three days after being nailed to a cross—she was naturally a bit hesitant.

Finally, though, we could all see her big promotion was getting close. My father had moved to the fold-out sofa in the living room while Mother mostly stayed in the hospital bed that held pride of place in the family room. Grandchildren and great-grandchildren sat on the ends, dangling their feet and watching the large screen television, or wandering in and out from the backyard pool. After the little ones were asleep, the rest of us sat around her big bed, drinking pitchers of margaritas or Tom Collins, and playing pinochle/accusing each other of cheating, while Mother sucked down spoonfuls of Baileys and morphine.

One afternoon, the phone rang and it was Mother's banker, asking how she was doing. With all the yelling and laughing, one sister took the call into the other room. "She's good. She's drinking Baileys and cheating at pinochle."

He cleared his throat a few times. "The thing is, we have a lady here wanting to cash a check for her granddaughter, who she says was your mother's nurse. The check is drawn on your mother's account for several thousand dollars."

"Um, could you hold a minute please?"

One of my sisters looked up from the pile of limes she was slicing. She remembered a young aide who had come for a day, but left early when she got a call saying her grandmother had died. In collegial respect for a fellow dying professional, Mother had insisted that my brother give her a ride home. We got out my parents' checkbook and looked at the register. Nothing had been written in quite a while. "What's the check number?"

It was from the box of unused checks up in their study. He promised to notify the police and we said goodbye.

Cards forgotten, we all sat around discussing the special kind of *cojones* it would take to steal from a dying woman, even one who'd been at it for thirty-plus years. Mother felt sorry for the girl who had just lost her grandmother, until I told her Granny had miraculously come back from the grave to help cash the check. I think my mother was intrigued.

While Mother consoled herself with sips of Baileys, the rest of us decided this was a job for mojitos. The doorbell rang, and two polite young police officers introduced themselves. I asked if they wanted to come in, and they looked grave. "No, we heard about your mother and don't want to disturb your family at a time like this. We can talk out here."

I closed the door on a loud accusation of dastardly card-deeds and accompanying burst of laughter. "Yes?"

They explained they needed us to file a complaint, and to provide details about our contact with the young woman. She had already told them that although she'd been sent by an agency, my mother was apparently so grateful for whatever services she'd provided in her few hours of aide work that she pressed the check into her reluctant hands. They showed me a copy of the check, and the illegible signature could have been Mother's. It could also have been Ghengis Khan's.

I explained that Mother was dying (I didn't say for how long), and we'd all gathered to be at her bedside. She did have full-time health aides, but the agency sent over subs sometimes when one of the others couldn't be there. This one hadn't even been there a full day.

The older officer had a lot of questions for me. His younger companion was extremely polite, but his eyes kept flicking over to the big picture window whenever a particularly loud burst of guffaws and/or accusations rang out.

The door behind me swung open to reveal one of my sisters with a pitcher of mojitos and some glasses. A niece took her arm and whispered in her ear, as peals of mirth rang out behind them. I closed the door and met two impassive faces.

I returned their stares. What I wanted to say was that in listing her seven stages of grief—at least as it was practiced in our family—Dr. Elisabeth Kübler-Ross left out the manic, inappropriate humor stage. And the mojitos.

I settled for an attempt at dignity. "Everyone grieves in their own way." Then I closed the door and took the glass my sister held out. Best mojito ever.

That night, we all pitched in to help with the cooking. I made my special garlic roast chicken, forgetting Mother never ate garlic. The smell spread through the house, and she surprised us by coming to the table for dinner. As usual, she was laughing and making death jokes—"Better have seconds now, because I'll be dead broke later, if that girl cashed more checks. Or maybe just dead."

Everyone marveled at the way she rallied, joked, and ate my chicken. That night, when it was my turn to sit with her, she asked about each of my children. After I filled her in, she sighed, "I think that's good enough."

Even Mother had to be right eventually. The next morning, after the funeral home's hearse had taken her away, one of my sisters turned to me. "It was your garlic chicken. I think you killed her."

EPILOGUE: The night of her funeral, I woke up to find Mother sitting on the end of my bed. I asked her if she was okay, and she said she was just waiting for my father, who was always late. "Maybe you should make him some of that chicken."

She was still laughing as I drifted back to sleep.

I'm not sure how other families do it, but we had team shirts, family jokes, a theme—<u>The Big Chill</u> meets <u>Waking Ned Devine</u>—and lots of Baileys.

❖ ❖ ❖

Chapter 49: Bang The Drum Slowly

A Republican can love a Democrat but lock up the knives during election years.

Once upon a time (actually, it was February 23, 1952), a lovely girl named Genevieve married a handsome guy named Bob, even though he was a Republican. Despite epic spoon-flinging election year 'discussions' and a profound aversion to hugging, the next six decades produced ten children, nine sons-and-daughters-in law, twenty-nine grandchildren (plus assorted partners), and three great-grandchildren, plus deeply affected the lives of many more.

Growing up on the south side of Chicago as one of eleven children, Bob absorbed several critical life lessons.

- The Notre Dame fight song is an appropriate soundtrack for every important life event.

- Mayors are named Daley, cities are run by machines, and clout means... well if you have to ask, you don't have it.

- Also, carry jumper cables. Always.

After a few detours for service in the Army Air Force during World War II, followed by an engineering degree (Notre Dame, of course), Bob and Gen moved to California, where he continued to pass along life lessons to his growing family.

- Politics? A Republican can love a Democrat but lock up the knives during election years.

- <u>Multi-tasking?</u> If there was a California mission within a hundred miles, Bob would stop, deal out head-scarves to his eight daughters (or, if the scarves ran out, a spare kleenex and a bobby pin), and 45-minutes later he was stacking scarves and ticking the 'done' box on his top three priorities—family, religion, and education.

- <u>Travel?</u> From Big Basin redwoods and Santa Cruz beaches to cross-country expeditions, Bob drove all curves at top speed, often while using both hands to refill his pipe or light his cigar. Actually, his mountain driving inspired more fervent religious experiences for his passengers than every mission in California combined.

- <u>Strangers?</u> Bob never met one. He knew that everyone from colleagues to toll booth attendants would want to hear about his ten kids. In detail.

- <u>Success?</u> Bob collected the trophies of his victory over forty-plus years of tuition payments in his proudest possession, the display cabinet containing the mugs from all ten kids' universities.

But the most important life lesson he taught us was love. Love doesn't require hugs or kisses or even words. Sometimes love is the old cars you keep repairing, the toilets you keep unplugging, the tuition bills you keep paying, the vacations and new cars you keep putting off. It's making and sharing the perfect Tom Collins with your wife and anyone else who happens by at the end of the day. It's those tears you shed (proudly) at each of your children's weddings. And it's walking your guests to their car at the end of their visit, and then standing and waving until they are out of sight.

Bob, now we are honored and so grateful to be the ones waving you out of of sight as you leave to join Gen. No hugging.

◆ ◆ ◆

Chapter 50: It Really Was A Swell Funeral

It was a swell funeral that brought us together. I was in college in Chicago when my mother told me one of my cousins had taken up residence in the Home For Unwed Nurses next to the university's hospital. Naturally, I avoided her.

It wasn't just that I had plenty of spare cousins. (Although my Irish-Catholic forebears had followed the commandment to "Be fruitful and multiply" so enthusiastically that a relative with fewer than six kids was considered practically childless. There may have been novenas.)

It wasn't just that she came from an upscale suburb. (Although I was sure the girls there ironed their designer jeans and shaved their legs daily. Even in winter.)

It wasn't just that she moved to my neighborhood. (Although voluntarily moving to Hyde Park on the South Side of Chicago seemed to me like voluntarily hitting yourself over the head. The best thing you can say about it is how good it feels when you stop. The worst thing is after a while, your head is a real mess.) I couldn't figure out why anybody would choose Hyde Park when they could go someplace more pleasant, like a war zone.

No, the real reason was that she was beautiful. Her whole family was beautiful. As for my own family, Sister #6 nailed it. "Out of all ten of us, I'm the best looking one and I'm only cute."

Luckily, glamour was not a prerequisite to a successful social life in Hyde Park. This was only partly because there was no social life in Hyde Park. Did you ever wonder what became of that grade-grubbing, geeky nerd in your high-school class? Well, they say home is the place where, when you go there, they have to take you in. Hyde Park took us in.

We called it "The Life of the Mind". But let's face it—the mind doesn't throw nearly as good a party as the body, especially those parts of the body that make 99% of college kids' social decisions. In other college towns during my university years, kids with normal social lives were out getting arrest records. We were out getting mugged. My only brush with the law came the night I was walking home late from Jimmy's, Hyde Park's sole college bar. A squad car pulled up next to me. Over the loudspeaker boomed the Mephistophelian voice of another of my cousins: *"BARB, DOES YOUR MOTHER KNOW YOU'RE OUT AT THIS HOUR?"*

So naturally, when I heard that Miss America in a nurse's cap had moved to the neighborhood, I greeted the news with the enthusiasm usually reserved for active plague carriers. She was no more anxious to meet me. The first person she saw when she got to Hyde Park was standing in the middle of the street having a heated argument (which he appeared to be losing) with himself about a dog. In Hyde Park, talking to yourself–and answering–is not uncommon. It might mean you are a Nobel Prize-winning scientist. It might mean you are a rubber-room refugee. Sadly, it often might mean both.

Soon after this, she met some people who beat her with pointed sticks for refusing their request that she hand over her bike. What really bothered her was the universal Hyde Park response that this was her fault for not having cash for the muggers. The first thing Hyde Park residents learned was to always carry an extra ten dollars for the mugger. (I did hear of a case where an impoverished graduate student's mugger agreed to take a check...)

She was also disconcerted by the main topic of conversation at social gatherings. Roaches. You could guess one's academic discipline from their preferred methods of roach removal. These ranged from the hard scientists employing biological warfare/chemical agents/engines of destruction, to the philosophers who questioned the roaches' reality.

But after about six months of increasing maternal pressure on both sides, we finally agreed to meet for dinner. Each of us brought along a friend whose sole function was to rescue us from potentially flagging conversation with a reminder about the three term papers/nursing shifts due in the morning. Don't judge. Escape was hard in those prehistoric days BC (before cellphones).

To The Hub, our worry about finding conversational common ground is the funniest part of the story. When you come from large families like both mine and my cousin's, you learn to talk early and often, and to follow at least three simultaneous conversations. He thinks if Eve had been in our family, we would never have left the Garden of Eden because the snake wouldn't have gotten a word in edgewise.

And, in fact, the friends listened in horrified silence as we got on the subject of my grandmother's swell funeral.

"Did you know about the Great-Uncle who was too cheap to rent a hotel room, so he slept in grandma's bed?"

"How about the one who snuck out of the funeral early so she could put her name on Grandma's things that she wanted?"

"Can you believe how smashed those cousins got at the restaurant after?"

"And who were those two swabbing each other's tonsils out in the hall?"

"Too bad Grandma missed it–she would have had a ball."

We got through the entire evening without ever mentioning roaches. I forgave her for being beautiful; she forgave me for being a Hyde Parker. I taught her my method for roach removal; she taught me how to apply eye-liner. We ended up sharing an apartment until she got married.

And we owe it all to Grandma's swell funeral.

◆ ◆ ◆

Chapter 51: 22 Letters That Spell "HERO"

"What do you want on the headstone?"

The funeral director was going down a list of decisions we needed to make for my father's funeral, and I thought I was doing fine until that one. As a veteran, my father had arranged to be buried with my mother at the National Cemetery in nearby Riverside, California. In fact, my parents had already made almost all the arrangements, so we didn't have that much to decide. Until we heard the funeral director say, "The National Cemetery only allows names, dates, and a twenty-two-character inscription."

Seriously? We were supposed to sum up their lives in twenty-two characters (including spaces and punctuation)?

You have to understand. I have nine brothers and sisters. That means ten different opinions on what those twenty-two letters could contain.

At first, we went for historical accuracy— *"Those damn kids!"*.

Then a score card— *"1 wife+10 kids=32 grands"*.

We tried channeling my mother's... unique... humor— *"OK boys, let her RIP"*.

We even thought about the texting approach— *"(-<-) & shhh @ last"*.

It wasn't that we hadn't thought about our parents' legacy. In fact, just days before he died I read my Veterans Day blog post "Do You Know A Hero?" to my father. The last time I saw him smile was when I called him my hero.

With both Memorial Day and Father's Day coming up without my parents, I was thinking about that grave and the beautiful cemetery around it. My brother just sent me a picture of the headstone, with the sedately accurate 22-character sum of their legacy *"Welcomed Laughed Loved"* (plus, of course, two little bottles-whiskey for him and Bailey's for her). I pictured them there, surrounded by fellow veterans.

This Memorial Day, I'm so grateful, once again, for my father and all those who answered their country's call. And especially, I'd like to thank those who gave up their lives so that others could have their family members long enough to argue about those twenty-two letters.

So how do you say hero in twenty-two characters? In Riverside National Cemetery, it's written two hundred thousand ways.

❖ ❖ ❖

PART 8: WRITING

♦♦♦

Chapter 52: Writer or Supermom?

"Dear Barb," a reader asks, "How did you become a writer?"

Well, Dear Reader, it's not a pretty story. My parents were too poor to afford guardian angels for each of their ten children, so I went through childhood with two little guardian social workers sitting on my shoulders. One had a three-piece suit and a briefcase, the other had sensible shoes and a diaper bag.

Age 5: *Guardian-SW#1*: "Barb, you can use your school years to construct a foundation of cultural values, human experience and long division on which to build a successful career as a best-selling writer."

Guardian-SW#2: "Be a super-mommy, be a super-mommy!"

Age 17: *Guardian-SW#1*: "Barb, here in college you can share the lives and ideas of the greatest writers of history."

Guardian-SW#2:"Be a super-mom, be a super-mom!"

Age 21: *Guardian-SW#1*: "Barb, you can walk on the moon, achieve racial and sexual equality, invent a $1.49 pantyhose that looks like silk and never runs, and write about all of it. And, thanks to the pill, you'll never have to swab a baby's behind."

Guardian-SW#2: "Be a super-mother, be a super-mother!"

Age 28: *Guardian-SW#1*: Barb, you have a great writing career, car, and sex life. One more thing and you'll have it all. Be a super-mother!"

Barb: "Hey, what happened to *Guardian-SW#2?*"

Guardian-SW#1: "I took over her caseload when her job was cut during that last round of celestial downsizing. So she's gone back to get a PhD in Women's Studies at Berkeley, and I'm about to take maternity leave myself."

◆ ◆ ◆

Another reader writes, "Dear Barb, How do you know if you should be a writer or a super-mother?"

Dear Reader, I'm glad you asked me that.

In 1894, William O. Atwater of the U.S.D.A. offered nutrition advice about basic food groups for free. In 1992, the U.S. Government spent over $1.5 million to convert his nutrition information into a poster with pyramid-shaped color graphics.

[No, Dear Reader, I didn't forget your question, I just get paid by the word. Now, watch this.]

Now that they've got the nutrition issue settled, the government will obviously be looking for another project to fund. So I'm offering them The Super-Mother Quiz. Of course, while I wouldn't dream of charging the Feds for such essential information, I will obviously have to ask them for $1.5 million to cover the cost of the color graphics. In the meantime, I'm offering you, Dear Reader, a chance to be one of the first to test your maternal qualifications by taking the following quiz.

The Super-Mother Quiz

Check Each Category Which Applies:

_____1.   *You employ the wisdom of Solomon to adjudicate a dispute over a Tinkertoy, but you answer questions about universal truths with, "Because I'm the mother and I say so."*

_____2.   *When you sing along with "Chicken Lips and Lizard Hips" in the car, not only are you alone, but you know the words. All of them.*

_____3.   *In dressing for your professional role as a MFTAKU (Mobile Field Trashcan and Kleenex Unit), you find that the latest Gucci or Versace lacks the sartorial cachet of the "Chocolate Chips" Desert Storm uniforms.*

_____4.   *You rock back and forth, one hip permanently higher than the other even when the only thing you're cradling is the phone.*

_____5.   *Your walls display framed works of art featuring stick figures whose arms and legs protrude directly from their heads.*

_____6.   *You drive to another store during a blizzard because the first one is out of your child's preferred brands of peanut-butter or hotdogs.*

_____7.   *You wrote your college term paper ("Feminist Influences in the Periodic Table of the Elements") in two hours and 45 minutes, but you stay up until dawn assembling your third-grader's science fair project ("Our Friend the Electron").*

_____8.   *You have just returned from scuba-diving in New Zealand and you're trying to decide how to spend all your leisure time. In your living room (which is filled with antique furniture, first editions, and your notes for the photo-essay book on your growing world-class collection of early Dan Quayle speeches), you set this quiz amid the handblown glass collectibles on the glass-topped coffee table over the white carpet while you sit on the white leather couch sipping (red) wine and considering each answer.*

SCORING: If you checked #8, congratulations! You are obviously ready for the enriching and fulfilling experience of super-motherhood. We here at the Super-Motherhood Quiz recommend you have several children, preferably male, as quickly as possible.

If you checked 1-7, super-motherhood is definitely not for you, and you're destined for a career with indefinite hours, low pay, little recognition, and occasionally getting thrown up on—professional writer (or Mom). Have you given any thought to the Women's Studies program at Berkley?

❖ ❖ ❖

Chapter 53: Blockbuster

"This is not a novel to be tossed aside lightly. It should be thrown with great force." —Dorothy Parker

In his book, *Writing the Blockbuster Novel* (Writer's Digest books, 1994) Altert Zuckerman lists the blockbuster's two essential elements:

1. **The writing**. Blockbuster novels need larger-than-life characters, a dramatic question, an exotic setting, and high stakes.

2. **The $500,000 advance**. Blockbuster novelists need LARGE checks.

Since my life as a #1 has given rise to my need for #2, I've decided to write a blockbuster best seller. While some critics feel the public demands originality, others believe that authors should only write about extraordinary events they have personally experienced. However, this does not explain the continued success of popular fiction authors such as Robert Fulghum, Victoria's Secret Catalog, Rush Limbaugh, or the United States Senate.

Therefore, for those readers who demand the cutting-edge of literary offerings with the comfort of familiarity, I offer excerpts from my new and very original opus: *"BARB'S LOVE STORY: NOW THAT DIRTY HARRY'S GONE WITH WHAT THE WIND BLEW IN FROM CASABLANCA, WHO'S GOING TO PICK UP THE STAR WARS AND PIECES ALL OVER THE PLAYROOM IF I'M HOMELESS ALONE UNDER THE BRIDGES OF COOK COUNTY?"*

DISCLAIMER*: Some thoughts and dialogue attributed to figures in this* *narrative were created by the author, based on such research and her knowledge of relevant people, places, and things.* **

> **   *(My publishers may demand a disclaimer like the one attached to Joe McGinniss' book, "The Last Brother" just because McGinniss quotes thoughts he "...sensed Teddy [Kennedy] must have been feeling." Therefore, those passages which may not be strictly autobiographical, such as the thoughts I sensed God must have been feeling, have been marked with* **).

Barb, a tall, slender, striking blonde, was sitting with her four tall, slender, healthy blonde children on her striking blonde** sofa in her immaculate, tastefully decorated home reading them Kant's *Critique of Pure Reason*.

> **   *(Okay, so the sofa is actually beige. Sue me.)*

Suddenly, Mars went retrograde. In the eerie silence which followed, Barb noticed that not only was water flooding out of the bathroom, but she was a lot shorter and darker. Her skin started to break out too. "Mama, our throats hurt," whimpered her children.

"Fiddle-dee-dee," she replied. "We'll cry tomorrow. right now, I'll have to fix the toilet." After a brief meditation on the sacred texts—*The Reader's Digest Book of Home Repair*—Barb groaned. "Plumber's snakes... Why does it always have to be snakes?" Soon, she had to admit defeat. "Swim toward the car, kids, and we'll go for help." But as the car wheezed slowly out of the garage, Barb knew there was only one man who could help her. "We'll have to get it to Rick's Car Repair Americain & Foreign." As they arrived, she heard Rick murmur, "Of all the car repair joints in all of the midwest, why did she have to end up here?"

"You're the only one who can help my carburetor. Please do whatever it takes to get us out of here," Barb whispered meaningfully when she handed over her credit card. As she left, Rick was telling the Visa people, "This could be the beginning of a beautiful friendship."

Arriving home, penniless and alone (the kids took her last $20 and all her two-fer coupons to ChuckUp-Cheeze, and her Prince Charming was, of course, attending a work conference in a foreign country), Barb knew there was only one thing left to try. "I'll call the Appliance Astrologer."

Half an hour later, the repairman had arrived. [**Fiction, remember we're talking fiction here...] His ruggedly handsome features creased with concern, he read the charts of the dishwasher (which had water flowing out of it) and the ice-maker (which didn't).

"Are you feeling lucky today?" he asked Barb.

"Don't try to spare me," she replied. "I can take the truth. How much longer do they have?"

"Well, I did dig out this wad of Plaster of Paris which had blocked your sink. But the fact is that the universe is against you—Mars is retrograde until March 5, and with your sign being Virgo it means that appliances and communication will be in danger till then." He glanced apprehensively at the VCR and the microwave blinking "12:00, 12:00, 12:00...", while in the background the toilet ran softly. Holding his appliance-scrying crystal between them, he started backing toward the door.

"No, don't leave me like this," begged Barb. "What if the stove goes too?"

"We'll always have the Plaster of Paris," he said as he repeatedly tried to start his truck in her driveway. "And if you need me, just whistle. You know how to whistle, don't you?"

"Does this mean the phone's broken too?" Barb sobbed. "But... I've just realized that it's my portable phone I truly love. What will I do?"

"Frankly, my dear," his voice floated back as he drove off into the sequel,"I don't give a darn."

◆ ◆ ◆

Chapter 54: Writer Wanted: Experience With Toilet Training, Personal Plumbing, & Bad Vacation Choices

"What do you do?"

"I get to know fascinating people on an intimate level. I live with them until I know their very souls. Then I torture and sometimes kill them."

I could have said that to the nice passport control officer at Glasgow Airport. But some people tend to take that the wrong way, so I just said, "I'm a writer. I make up lies for a living. It's kind of like being a Russian troll except they earn more—but at least nobody blames me for Trump." We agreed that neither of us knew George R.R. Martin, one of us liked the books, one of us liked the *Game of Thrones* show, and I went on my way.

But I was thinking about my resume, especially because I've started getting (completely unsolicited!) daily emails with subject line *Jobs: Writer*. Apparently there's a pharmaceutical-dependency issue in the recruitment industry because the sender thinks I'd be a perfect candidate for some of the following opportunities:

- *Retail Strategy and Change*: Since my retail strategy consists of spending everything I've got including any small change I can dig out of the couch cushions, I'd have to say I'm qualified.

- *Administration and Communications Officer*: I raised four kids without getting a criminal record, even when Child#2 was learning to drive. Nailed.

- *Traceability Coordinator*: Since the maternal uterus is obviously a tracking device that ensures I'm the only one in the house who knows where anything is, I'm also a shoe-in for this one.**

- *Helpline Advisors*: With four kids, I'm an advice expert, whether by phone, email, Google, Messenger, Telegram, etc.) *[NOTE: if this job requires Snapchat, though, I'm not a fit. My kids say mamas aren't allowed to Snap.]*

- *Business Intelligence*: After about a bazillion years (give-or-take) as a corporate executive, I can honestly say that term is an oxymoron. So I'm guessing this one also involves Russian trolls.

- *Dutch-speaking Inside Sales Rep.* and *French-speaking, plus Italian-speaking Customer Service Advisor*: Echt niet. En aucune façon. Non c'è modo. No way.

  ** *The Traceability Coordinator job description also listed its Main Job Requirement as "speaking, writing and understanding good spoken and written English language." There's a test.*

It would have been great if someone had given me a test 30+ years ago when I started my big job as The Mom.

Help Wanted: Mom. *Expanding organization seeks Director. Qualifications: must know how to put toilet paper on spindle, prepare creative and interesting dishes for staff to refuse if they don't involve the words 'peanut butter' and serve as walking Kleenex to small staff members. On-call 24/7, no pay, no sick leave, no chance of promotion. Job security, annual recognition breakfast, company car.*

There are aspects of parenting that weren't covered in my job contract when I promised to 'love and honor' and were never mentioned by our natural childbirth teacher either. Although the latter went into alarming detail about the Miracle of Birth, she never even touched on the technical difficulties to come. Take, for example, explaining toilet procedures to a barely verbal little person with a completely different set of internal plumbing.

After my son had successfully sent many Cheerios to a watery grave (I threw handfuls of Cheerios into the toilet with the instructions that he should 'sink the ships'), he naturally wanted to demonstrate his newfound prowess at every opportunity. So we embarked on a theme tour—a plumbing comparison of public restrooms in every grocery and shop in the greater Central Illinois area. I soon discovered that while my son's personal equipment was handy for a hike in the woods, most public toilets were so high that someone three-foot-tall couldn't hope to stand and deliver. I've been known to balance him on the top of my feet —not an ideal arrangement when it involved the split-second attention span of

171

the average three-year-old male.

"You sure he can't wait?" our guides would typically inquire as they conducted us personally through wilderness grocery canyons of disposable diapers and sugar-intensive cereals, a mysterious territory few outsiders have ever penetrated. The guide would produce a key and wave us into the room labeled *"Employees Must Wash Hands"* where we would inhale the heady fumes of the 47 packets of cigarettes consumed during the last shift alone.

To protect us from the germs and disease spread by paper litter, signs also informed us, these restrooms were thoughtfully provided with electric hand-dryers installed by the Marquis de Sade. My son's horror of hand-dryers will someday provide gainful employment for his therapists, but at the time it usually resulted in our entire wet-handed party giving chase as he fled screaming in terror from the bathroom. I can only give thanks that employees of Child Protective Services rarely found their way into the depths of grocery storage.

The plumbing comparison did prove educational for his two older sisters. Because both were now literate, they spent their time studying the messages inscribed on the restroom walls, asking if we could call any of the phone numbers to see what kind of good time the referenced persons provided, and speculating on possible uses for the machine-vended items in designer pastel colors.

In my euphoria at venturing out in public for the first time since the year 1 BC (Before Children) without the minimal diapering supplies necessary to survive a minor world war, I became convinced our family was ready to combine the plumbing tour with a cross-country vacation.

Okay, so I've been wrong before.

In point of fact, we have a remarkable record as vacation companions. To date, everybody we ever vacationed with had gotten a divorce within the following year. This time we decided to play it safe and go with friends who've been together for almost twenty years.

The first day at the beach, I could see that one of my friends was troubled. So I asked her to reassure me that she was simply suffering from a minor form of terminal cancer which wouldn't interfere with our vacation. No such luck. That week provided the novel experience of sharing a small house with a large group including two soon-to-divorce adults treating each other like snail phlegm.

Somehow we tore ourselves away and headed for a few days of camping in the Smokies. We could only stay for a short time, however, because as we arrived we were informed that it is a federal crime to bathe there. We assumed the Feds were counting on the eau d'campers to provide bear-repellant, but the ranger explained that the soap residue from the approximately 500 campers per day would send the fish straight from their erstwhile *[NB: I've always wanted to use erstwhile in a post]* pristine streams to that big pond in the sky.

While the Ranger couldn't personally document the arrest of any ripe campers sneaking a scrub, we decided not to take any chances. We stayed until our clothes began to walk around by themselves and then made a dash for home.

As we drove toward the flat lands of Central Illinois, we reflected that word would probably get out about vacationing with us. But just in case, I have a position opening for next July.

Help Wanted: Travel Companions. *Must have barely minimal hygiene requirements, a stable personal situation, and potty-trained kids.*

◆ ◆ ◆

Chapter 55: Rip My Old Friend...Or Not.

This week I mourned the loss of my closest confidant.

We've been together for over six years. When the Hub was away, I'd sometimes wake up to realize my old friend had been in bed with me all night. (Occasionally with some drool where I'd fallen asleep.) He kept me company in Russia, India, Australia, across the US and Canada, and in many of the countries of Europe.

And I'd poured out my heart to him. He knew every one of my secrets, held every book I'd ever written, every thought I'd recorded over the past six years. Lately, though, he hasn't been himself. He's been slowing down, occasionally forgetting things. Of course, so have I.

Then came the morning last week when I noticed that his peripherals weren't responding.

I knew he wouldn't want me to prolong his agony, but he held it together long enough for one last backup. The expert at the Genius Bar shook his head, and closed my old friend's cover for the last time.

I left the store with his replacement, feeling guilty and excited. My old friend and I had been together for so long. Was I ready for a new relationship already? Or would this just be a rebound fling? At home, I connected the peripherals, turned on the new guy, and stood back. He hummed gently, sucked in the backup data, and lit up the monitor, while I held my breath. Would we get along? Would he be good in my bed?

"Restore from backup?"

It was scary, but I clicked *yes*. More humming.

Then, before my eyes, my old friend rose from the dead. He's back—bigger, stronger, faster, with a shiny unmarked face and more memory. He did not go gently into that dark place with no 1s and 0s. Nope, he's got a much bigger drive and he's ready to party. And... I hope this doesn't make me sound shallow, but it's true. Size matters. My New Old Friend is just so big...and powerful.

If only that worked for people too.

♦ ♦ ♦

The End? Never!

Your turn! I'd love to hear what you think of these little essays. Please let me know if you've had similar experiences, or any other thoughts, comments, or suggestions you might want to share.

Of course, you'll have my undying gratitude if you leave a review online. But I'd also be thrilled to have you visit my blog at https://barbtaub.com or send email to barbtaub@gmail.com.

And above all, thank you for sharing your reading time with me. —Barb

◆ ◆ ◆